"Fit In or Stand Out is ... press and use your t... sightful, recognizable and sharp exposure of the daily ...... between conformity and staying true to your unique Talent. A gift for everyone who wants to unlock their individual power, creativity, and impact every day a bit more.
MARGA MATHIJSSEN, VP Marketing at Unilever

"Anke has done a masterful job at taking challenging concepts and making them actionable. I've shrunk to fit in and it feels like wearing someone else's clothes...that are too tight and not at all my style. But I didn't have words to describe that until reading this book. However, my limiting tendencies are no match for the joy and freedom I've found in letting my Talent shine. I'm a Guide. Claiming that sacred identity makes me feel stronger and bolder. And we need bold women now more than ever. So get this book and I'll see you in the arena."
LORI HARRIS, Sr Director Global Fortune 100

"An important, well-researched book on the power of Talent and uncovering hidden potential. Eloquently, Anke Tusveld, invites us to revitalize our organization using our authentic Talent—very valuable in a fast-paced, agile world in which everyone seems to be paralyzed by their tendency to stick to "what we were used to."
MENNO LANTING, Author Connect and The Disruptive Paradox

"This book really had me thinking about my Unique Talent. An in-depth read in this fast paced world, Anke Tusveld provides hundreds of questions and highly relevant examples. This book is for anyone who wants to amplify their authentic leadership style, without the usual gimmicky quick fix."

AN CLAES, Fortune 100 Global Executive

"It's remarkable, how Anke Tusveld, step by step, leads the reader towards standing out and using their Talent. Using incredible accurate words, she shines the light on the magnificent impact you make when taking your Talent as your starting point. It's a generous book full of wisdom, elaborate examples and vivid metaphors. Definitely a must-read!"

BERNADET HAVEMAN, Entrepreneur (Droom van Zwolle) and Talent Coach

"Anke brings to this book a wealth of wisdom wrapped in useful, applicable concepts that create space to discover one's innate strengths and most importantly, ways to bring them to life."

NICOLE FLINTERMAN, Mindfulness educator and coach at Unfolding Mindfulness

Copyright © 2018 by Anke Tusveld.

All rights reserved. No part of this publication may be reproduced, distributed or transmitted in any form or by any means, including photocopying, recording, or other electronic or mechanical methods, without the prior written permission of the publisher, except in the case of brief quotations embodied in critical reviews and certain other noncommercial uses permitted by copyright law. For permission requests, write to InterAgri Publishers.

Cover Design and illustrations : Holly Amaoko
Author photo credit: Chelsea Perri

Publisher's Note: Names, characters, places, and incidents have been changed to ensure client's anonymity. Any resemblance to actual people, living or dead, or to businesses, companies, events, institutions, or locales is completely coincidental.

Ordering Information: Quantity sales. Special discounts are available on quantity purchases by corporations, associations, and others. For details, contact the author at www.anketusveld.com

Fit In or Stand Out/ Anke Tusveld -- 1st ed.
ISBN 978-978-0-9998987-2-7

FIT IN
OR
STAND OUT

USE YOUR TALENT

WHEN IT MATTERS

ANKE TUSVELD

InterAgri Publishers

United States

"What if the so-called inviolable bounds
drawn by convention
turn out to be nothing else but
innocuous chalk lines."

– Louise von Salome

Contents

One — Invitation to Learn 1

PART I FITTING IN 23

Two — Why do we want to Fit In? 27

Three — Benefits of Fitting in at Work 45

Four — Sacrifices of Fitting in at Work 51

Five — Letting Go of our Masks to Hide Ourselves 61

PART II STANDING OUT 89

Six — Everyone Can Be Outstanding—Yes, Everyone 93

Seven — Identifying our Authentic Talent 121

Eight — Using our Talent, Especially When It Really Matters 129

Nine — The Courage to Lead from Within 143

Ten — The Courage to Create 169

Eleven — The Courage to Connect 205

Acknowledgements 232

Beyond the Book 234

"Consider yourself lucky if
you have heard
a whispering voice in your mind
asking:
Is this really what I want? Is this all I've got?
Who am I really?"

ONE — INVITATION TO LEARN

When we slowly but surely are groomed into something we are not.

Cara's honesty struck me. She had lost control of her life's steering wheel. Her primary focus on other people's needs had replaced any sense of really knowing who she was herself. In one of our sessions she realized:

> I feel I have moved away from that spontaneous, passionate alive person that I was. I spend so little time on identifying what I want in life—from career to hobbies to even how I wish to spend my time on the weekend.

> I feel like I am waiting for life to happen to me rather than actually steering myself deliberately in the direction I want to go. This seems so ironic when I am interested in so many things of such a broad nature, but I am just not doing them.

Life was happening to her as she ran like a madwoman to keep up, but she was starting to realize she wanted to get off of that hamster wheel. But how? What was the alternative? What was her purpose, and what made her happy? These were questions that, deep down, she might have known the answers to, but having lost complete touch with her own truth, she could no longer answer them.

If you'd met Cara at work, you wouldn't have known things were bothering her so much. She was an ambitious business consultant with a career on the rise, seeming to tick all the boxes. She rocked at fitting in perfectly, but in order to do so, she felt she had to hide her true colors from the outside world. Sadly, her fear of being herself largely impacted what she had to offer to make a difference in her world.

Cara[1] is not the only person to unintentionally choose to *change herself* over *being herself*. Over 80 percent of the hundreds of professionals in leadership development training programs I facilitate deal with the delicate dance of fitting in and standing out. Both are important to career success. However, most of the time, the balance between the two is lost. These professionals are secretly insecure, but they comprehensively cover their anxiety by wearing a mask, especially in cases when they're meeting with people they look up to or when the stakes are especially high, for example during annual budget meetings or performance reviews.

In wearing that mask, they lose their ability to be autonomous and creative at work. Despite the fact that they have relatively successful careers, they feel exhausted by pretending to be someone they are not and are fed up with constantly comparing themselves to others. They desire to become themselves again: authentic, confident, and independent leaders who make a significant difference and who are able to connect on a deeper level in a fast-paced, demanding corporate culture. They desire to leave a legacy.

---

[1] To ensure my clients' privacy, all names and details are changed throughout the book.

To be ourselves in a world that is trying to make us like everyone else is one of our biggest challenges in life and work. Slowly but surely, we are groomed into something we are not, starting with school, the first step for many people en route to a successful career. It's as if we each order the same "how to be perfect" box online, and then we hide in that box for years. Over time, we build a gilded-guard because we think others won't think we are enough without it. We accelerate in the ability to fit in because of our inborn desire to belong.

I, myself, am no different. I fully understand this course of events, because I lived in the same fitting-in fog. I even remember the exact moment I decided I wanted to fit in. It was an afternoon, and I was surrounded by other high-schoolers who were all winding their way down the narrow path next to the school building. I stood still in the middle of this noisy stream of people and was struck by my thoughts. My hands clamped to hold my backpack in my attempt to control my mind. *I want to fit in. I am fed up with looking up to the popular kids. I want to belong.* That moment marked two decades of fitting in. I became great at knowing how to dress appropriately, knowing what to say, knowing when to laugh and knowing who to best connect with.

It worked. My ability to blend in got me far. At university, I was selected for the popular extracurricular jobs, like running a discotheque for a year. Selected from thousands of applicants, I got to do an internship for a telecommunications company in Tokyo. In my career, I got along very well with clients and I was able to connect easily with people of different cultures, which was helpful for living and working abroad happily. In a sense, I am grateful that I took my desire to fit in seriously. But standing on that pathway next to my high school, I made one assumption that was fundamentally wrong.

What is the assumption that turns out to be fundamentally wrong?

I thought fitting in and wanting to belong meant that I had to turn into someone other than who I originally was. As if my "original me" wasn't good enough. In my attempt to be accepted by the outside world, I started to ignore my inside world. Since the moment I decided that I wanted to conform to "what's cool and what's not," I began living in a fog. At least, it felt like a thick fog surrounded me, because it felt like my senses were numbed. Sure, I was experiencing my life, but was I really in it?

My ability to fit in by changing myself took its toll. I decided to study at a technical university to prove that I was as intelligent as my brother and to meet the nonexistent demands of my parents. It might have made more sense for me to have studied psychology, a field that had fascinated me since an early age. As a result, despite having an exciting time during my university years, it seemed like I was living someone else's life. For a long time, I was able to numb my own feelings to satisfy other people's feelings and needs. My survival strategy was to reside in my head, which was, in hindsight, a pretty strong accomplishment since I originally am a person who thrives using her senses. Ultimately, I lost touch with what I truly felt or wanted. It was if, with the decision to fit in, I handed over my own sense of direction. My true colors tarnished and by blending in, I turned into someone bland.

Suppressed stressful feelings eventually caused hyperventilation, which became my wake-up call to finally escape the numbing fog. I cautiously started to add some of my own feelings to the mix, but I wasn't sure how to proceed and get off the hamster wheel with both feet. Those initial feelings weren't all kittens and rainbows. They hurt. I decided to choose a study of my own choice, a three-year Talent Development Academy at the Pulsar Institute[2]. They placed a mirror in front of me and asked: Who are you? What are your desires? What is your unique value to share with others? I didn't have any substantial answers because I was disconnected from myself.

From that moment on, things shifted, and I started to make my own choices. I found my way off of the hamster wheel. Step by step, my true colors emerged, and it felt extremely good despite the vulnerability that came with it. I escaped the numbing cloud and reconnected with passion, love, and life. I am still enjoying every step of it today. Learning how my mind worked, knowing what triggered my tendencies to fit in, and how to master those tendencies was lifesaving.

Identifying my own unique value helped me to quit looking up to others. What a relief! It opened my eyes to the amazing fact that we each have a specific and unique Talent, which is the root of our individual skills. When we identify and enable ourselves to express this Talent, we are able to make a significant change in our world.

The book you are about to read is my invitation to you to start standing out in your own way. I invite you to discover your signature strength and to bring that wonderful value into reality. Not only because the expression of this signature strength is the perfect antidote for your out-of-control fitting-in tendencies, but because your Talent, with a capital T, enables you to make a significant change in your world, small and big.

---

[2] The Pulsar Institute is based in the Netherlands. You can find more information in Dutch: www.pulsarinspireert.nl

Imagine yourself later in life sitting in your retirement home sharing personal stories and memories. Many people do not realize they have been living someone else's life until they are sipping cocktails with their fellow seniors and feel that nagging regret. Wouldn't it be great if those retirement home stories were all heart-fulfilling and significant events instead of regrets? Consider yourself lucky if you have heard a whispering voice in your mind asking: *Is this really what I want? Is this all I've got? Who am I really? What do I really stand for?*

Finding a balance between fitting in and standing out

We lose our ability to stand out in favor of our desire to fit in

The incredibly open look in my son's eyes touches me over and over again. He seems to receive everything with wonder and curiosity. Each time he finds a rock, he is amazed by its colors, stripes, weight, or shape. He totally loses track of time or his surroundings. Before his admiration for rocks existed, I never noticed how much beauty lies at our feet. One thing I envy more than ever is his wide-eyed wonder. I hope he keeps that curious outlook for as long as possible. But in theory, I know that eventually he'll partially lose this ability to look at the world without filters.

At some point, he will get chastised for expressing his enthusiasm, and he'll begin to hold back. It could be from being ignored, or from not having his excitement met, or from a non-intentional harsh remark. But somehow, he will get hurt in expressing his sincere enthusiasm, and he will be tempted to adjust his natural way of being, just like it happened to most of us. I truly hope he is able to maintain his unique spark and that open look in his eyes.

In *Creative Confidence*[3], writers David Kelley and Tom Kelley point to a moment in childhood development where we, as kids, start to judge ourselves and feel judged by others. We start to pay attention to the reactions around us and we stop dancing like nobody's watching. This is when our creativity is most vulnerable. We start reacting to the outside world, using cues to learn how to fit in and to escape being judged. In meeting life's demands, we trade in qualities that make us unique for ones that allow us to fit in and belong. We react instead of creating. At some point, we realize that we're not leading our own dance but are being led by the outside world.

How is your balance?

Take a moment to think about this: What colleague do you admire? Who is an example for you at work? I'm sure it's most likely someone who is authentic and who isn't afraid to show their true colors at key moments, rather than someone who excels at fitting in.

I'm curious. What is your balance? Take a look at the picture and

	FITTING IN	**STANDING OUT**
I say…	I should I have to	Let's I want to
I want to…	Be acknowledged Please others Meet expectations Belong	Make a difference Create significance Be proud of added value Connect
I am…	Pretending Secretly insecure Wearing a mask to cover my true feelings Matching myself with others Ignoring my own feelings	Authentic Confident Vulnerable Autonomous True to my own feelings

---

3 Tom Kelley and David Kelley, *Creative Confidence: Unleashing the Creative Potential Within Us All* (Crown Business, 2013)

answer honestly. Do you excel at fitting in? Do you live the expected life? Are you ignoring or postponing your dreams? Or maybe, you've lost sight on what your dreams and desires might be?

What do you hear yourself saying more often? I should, and ... I have to... or, let's, and ... I want to...? Are you driven to be acknowledged, to please others, and to meet expectations? How many times during your week do you feel so focused and in such a flow that you know you are really making a difference? And are you even aware of the value (your value) that you are adding or could be adding to your organization?

You might just be so skilled at hiding your true self that you don't have a clue what "your true self" even means. You might have lost track of what you really want and who you really are. And while you're working hard, you might have the feeling that there is some unused potential trapped inside you. Has the "I'm fine" mask that most of us wear become so comfortable that it's your default mode? What will be left if you unveil yourself? Who is behind the mask? What true potential hides behind the guard? Aren't you curious?

This book's content: What does it mean to stand out?

Author Michael Hall's children's book, *Red: A Crayon's Story*,[4] hits the nail on its head. He introduces Red, a crayon with a bright red label. This crayon is unhappy, since he tries his best to color as beautifully as his buddies, but none of his attempts lead to something extraordinary. First, everyone tries to help him by encouraging him to draw delicious red strawberries or fresh oranges by mixing colors with his yellow classmate. Red is heartbroken since his drawings turn

---

4 Michael Hall, *Red: A Crayon's Story* (Greenwillow Books, 2015)

out to be ugly-colored and he suffers from all the remarks others are making behind his back. Then a new friend looks beyond Red's label and asks him to draw a blue ocean. First, Red sadly replies, "I can't. I am Red." After some encouragement, Red gives it another try, although hesitantly. What happens? Red discovers he is actually blue beneath his red label. Now, he can draw everything blue from jeans to bells, from whales to berries, drawing beautifully without any effort, enjoying every drawing.

Standing out means finding the color we are wearing beneath our label and daring to start drawing like our life depends on it, enjoying every step on our way. It all starts with realizing and acknowledging that in our attempts to belong, we have changed ourselves and have been coloring with the wrong color, all the while growing another label from the outside.

Part I: *Fitting In* of this book answers every aspect of our tendencies to fit in.

- What makes us put on masks, conform, and adjust? What are the biological, cultural, and psychological reasons that make us want to fit in over and over, even beyond our own control?
- What are the benefits and what do we sacrifice while fitting in?
- How can we let go of our tendencies of fit in? Practice with three specific ways to shed self-doubts and self-judgments.

What color are we really from the inside? What if we could be as engaged in something as we were as children? What if we could kindle the spark within and not let it cease shining? What if we could make strong, autonomous decisions without hesitation? What if we would skip meeting imagined demands and save that energy for adding creative value in our own way? More and more, employers and customers have started looking for authentic and fresh approaches. They actually want us to bring our unique value to the table because "a copy is never as good as the original."

Part II: *Standing Out* explains what it actually means to stand out using our own authentic flavor.
- How can we stand out in significance? What is the role of our authentic Talent, the root of all our skills?
- What habits do we have to unlearn in order to stand out and make a difference?
- How can we uncover this hidden Talent? And how do we express our Talent?

Finally, after having colored with other colors for so long, what does it really mean to start being ourselves in an environment that doesn't seem to invite us to do so? Standing out in our own comfortable setting takes courage, but standing out in a not-so-comfortable setting like work is a whole different ballgame. However, the office is the ultimate practice area to master the art of standing out. Our automatic tendencies to adjust what we think other people expect are easily triggered in stressful environments. If, for example, we're operating in a corporate alpha-dominated culture and are joining "their" game: How can we learn the rules while not losing ourselves in the process? How can we take part and add our own flavor and shine at the same time?

The last three chapters of Part II dive deep into three areas of practice, the courage to lead from within, to create, and to connect. Each chapter will provide two specific Authenticity Enablers that will help us along the way of expressing our Talent without holding back.
- The Courage to Lead from within: What enables us to stay in the lead in a world full of distractions, fears, and seductions that keep us turning outwards focusing at our outside labels?

- The Courage to Create: What enables us to make a *difference* by doing things *differently*?
- The Courage to Connect: What enables us to really act on our Talent and stand out in a place that used to be threatening?

Until this point, your life may have looked like series of tryouts such that you're ready for the premiere. So, if you are curious to discover what magic you can bring to every situation, accept this invitation to learn. Learn how to get off that hamster wheel and out of that one-size-fits-all box. Learn what it takes to feel alive again and revitalize your surroundings with your Talent.

And remember, the learning process isn't always free from hardship—we all have to endure our fears when stepping outside of our comfort zone. Be encouraged by German diplomat, psychotherapist, and Zen master Karlfried Durckheim, who encapsulates this process by saying, "Everything that is alive is destined to evolve. But we will never become ourselves automatically. We will only become what we are if we take ourselves as serious as our most precious work."

The world is changing: Four (more) reasons to stand out

The most personal reason to identify your unique value is to live your life and not someone else's idea of it. However, on a larger scale, there are even more reasons to stand out and become more *you*. I want to introduce you to four developments that draw the bigger picture and explain why standing out is even more important now and in the future.

Reason 1: A Volatile, Uncertain, Complex, and Ambiguous (VUCA) world asks for a steady, authentic individual foundation

In the industrial era, employers were looking for standard approaches and saw employees as resources that had to fit into predestined boxes in order to perform standard tasks. But the industrial era is over—accomplishments and effects already achieved have been written in history books that are now collecting dust on dark bookshelves. We are living in a connected world, in a VUCA world.

VUCA is an acronym developed by the U.S. military after the collapse of the Soviet Union to describe a multipolar world: volatile, uncertain, complex, and ambiguous. We need to thrive within an unpredictable environment, making sense of complicated interdependencies in now globally-connected societies. In most working environments, we have to make decisions without having the whole picture, handling risks and uncertainties to one extent or another. Ambiguities challenge us to take a stand without a single truth backing us. We can no longer count on the seeming certainty and predictability of binary choices—capitalism versus communism, democracy versus autocracy. Choices and consequences are now far less clear than they once were. Turbulence, unpredictability, and complexity surround us.

To thrive in this VUCA world, we are in need of an anchor. We need an eye of the storm. Will your boss or CEO take on this role? Perhaps, although he or she will probably be busy developing his or her own personal stability to stand out in these ongoing storms of change. The times when we could solely rely on other people to make decisions for us in our jobs are over. Organizations have turned into large, complex networks, and it's almost impossible to be led by one single board. Our foundation needs to be stronger than ever to make decisions without being aware of the whole context. We need to change our focus from merely outwards (What do other people do?) to inwards (What do I stand for? What is my purpose? What do I think is important?).

Reason 2: Global challenges ask for creative minds, however...

We are in desperate need of innovative minds to create solutions to deal with scarce energy resources, migration due to conflicts and climate change, and a still-existing inequality among people. To innovate, we need creative and unique human beings with diverse opinions and ways of thinking. The time when the world required standardized people to perform standardized tasks is over. A large part of those jobs have been and will be computerized. However, are we and our organizations ready to do what it takes to really innovate and set foot on nonconforming pathways?

When I owned an innovation agency, *The Creativity Company*, with one of my best friends, we facilitated a large variety of creativity processes, from the creation of sustainable greenhouses to market introductions for Unilever, from new product development for large steel companies to new beer products. We also taught managers how to think creatively and how to facilitate creative thinking within their organizations. At the time, we mainly focused on teaching them creative thinking techniques and how to design creative thinking processes. Thousands of ideas were created, as well as lots of energy and buy-ins from colleagues, always important in innovation development. However, there was one thing that fascinated me and which eventually drove me into the area of personal development.

Despite the fact that we laid out dozens of creative thinking techniques, people didn't allow themselves to tap into their creativity fully. Their minds, or at least the minds of those who thought they weren't creative, remained rather inflexible. Their brains kept sticking to their default settings.

I now realize their minds were glued to their tendencies to fit in and therefore got stuck before they had even allowed themselves to imagine all the different possibilities. Those different possibilities scared them off.

IDEO founder David Kelley and his brother and IDEO partner, Tom Kelley, write in *Creative Confidence*[1] about how they encountered the same thing. They met professionals who would grab their smartphones when the process got fuzzy and unconventional, saying, "I'm just not the creative type." But when the clients stuck with it, they surprised themselves. When they developed a kind of ease with the uneasiness, they realized that they were more capable than they initially thought.

This is exactly what has always driven me in everything I do in work. People are so much more capable than they think. There is so much more in store than we think, if only we allow ourselves to develop ease with our uneasiness. Our creativity is essential to success in any discipline or industry. According to chief executives around the world, creativity is the most sought-after trait in leaders today.

Most companies are designed for efficiency and risk elimination. According to intensive research by Harvard Business School Professor Francesca Gino[5] involving more than 1,000 employees in a variety of industries, less than 10 percent said they worked in companies that regularly encourage nonconformity. In her article she states:

> *The pendulum has swung too far in the direction of conformity. For decades the principles of scientific management have prevailed. Leaders have been overly focused on designing efficient processes and getting employees to follow them. Now they need to think about when conformity hurts their business.*

To be successful and evolve, organizations need to strike a balance between a necessary structure and the freedom that helps employees do their best work.

Last weekend I was on the beach together with my dog. She desperately wanted to play and soon, she found a friend. But this dog was trained so well to obey the rules that he would stay seated, despite all the strategies my dog seduced him with. Have we also overtrained our professionals to conform to the existing rules? Are the lists of competencies they have to succeed in still allowing them to play, use their imaginations, and experiment? Why do companies invest a lot of time and money to create assessments for the "perfect leader" whose predefined scores on predefined capabilities might result in ho-hum outcomes? And if modern organizations value inno-

---

[5] Francesca Gino, "Let Your Workers Rebel," *Harvard Business Review* (2016)

vation, diversity, and creativity and therefore value constructive nonconformity, why are we still trying to shape our children into standardized molds with standardized tests?

Just like educational and organizational systems do not make it easy to develop our creativity, the Internet and social media also challenge that ability. Almost every moment we could use to reflect or just enjoy "being" has been taken over by looking at our devices and (usually) comparing ourselves to others. Our creativity can't develop when we're never engaged with our own sense of self. Deloitte's research[6] shows that the average American checks their phone 47 times per day. Within an hour of waking up, 89 percent reach for their phones. This is in addition to using our laptops and watching TV. A constant flow of information is entering our brains.

Nicholas Carr researches this phenomena in his book *The Shallows*.[7] He writes, "People will lose their abilities to employ a slower, more contemplative mode of thought." Research shows that as people get better at multitasking, they become less creative in their thinking. He continues, "What the Net seems to be doing is chipping away my capacity for concentration and contemplation. Whether I'm online or not, my mind now expects to take in information the way the Net distributes it: in a swiftly moving stream of particles. Once I was a scuba diver in the sea of words. Now I zip along the surface like a guy on a Jet Ski."

So, the ways we design our lives don't help us to become more creative and to use our unique Talent to make a difference. An enormous amount of information constantly enters our minds. We can use that for inspiration, but if we don't take time to process it, it

---

[6] "2017 Global Mobile Consumer Survey: US Edition", *Deloitte* (2017)

[7] Nicholas Carr, *The Shallows: What the Internet Is Doing to Our Brains* (WW Norton, 2010).

could actually stifle that creative potential. Finding ways to incorporate more moments of stillness and reflection will help us to avoid becoming shallow and instead, to cultivate creativity.

Reason 3: Diverse unique perspectives offer better solutions

Migration streams have led to multicultural societies and workplaces, and the world has further become a global village with the aid of advanced technology. It was just decades ago that women entered the workplace and added their unique perspectives. Traditional hierarchies have changed to allow for different age groups to work together more often. The workplace has become (and is becoming) more diverse than ever.

However, recent research of Deloitte[8] shows that 61% of people in the workplace still cover up our authentic aspects to fit in with the mainstream, certainly within groups that have been historically underrepresented, such as women (66%) and LGB individuals (83%). Why do we still find so much comfort in conformity?

Research was part of my Master's in Innovation Management. At the time, I was fascinated by creative problem-solving in groups. I decided to research which were more successful: homogenous or diverse groups. In other words, should you solve business problems using the experts within your organization, who might have more knowledge but are more inclined to conform and think inside the box? Or should you invite outsiders who are not hindered by existing knowledge and allow themselves to think outside the box?

The results showed two important facts: outsiders (or insiders with higher creative thinking abilities) resulted in better solutions

---

[8] Kenji Yoshinio and Christie Smith, "Uncovering talent - A new model of inclusion," *Deloitte* (2013)

because of the variety in their creative thinking skills and approaches. However, the groups with insiders resulted in a more successful implementation of the solutions, despite the fact that the solutions were less valuable.

First, these results led me to another definition of diversity. In order to really understand the value of diversity, we should look one step further than race, gender, or religious background. Research shows that the real value of diversity lies in whether a group is cognitively diverse—does their way of thinking differ? Do they have a different perspective or way of interpreting things? Do their problem-solving skills vary from the standard ones? In his book *The Difference* [9], Scott Page shares how, in some situations, a group of ordinary people can defeat a group of like-minded experts just by being more cognitively diverse.

Second, these results led me to my ongoing mission to transform workplaces into places that favor diversity versus fitting into the ruling cultures. Strong, homogenous cultures stifle the natural cognitive diversity in groups through the pressure to conform.[10] As Susan Cain, author of *Quiet*[11], states, "… today we make room for a remarkably narrow range of personality styles. We're told that to be great is to be bold, to be happy is to be sociable. We see ourselves as a nation of extroverts—which means that we've lost sight of who we truly are."

Dealing with like-minded people might seem easier and less threatening, but if you choose to go along with the flow and fit in, you harm your company's success by not bringing your unique value

---

[9] Scott E. Page, *The Difference: How the Power of Diversity Creates Better Groups, Firms, Schools, and Societies* (Princeton, 2007)

[10] Alison Reynolds and David Lewis, "Teams Solve Problems Faster When They're More Cognitively Diverse," *Harvard Business Review* (2017)

[11] Susan Cain, *Quiet: The Power of Introverts in a World That Can't Stop Talking* (Broadway Books, 2013)

to the table. Your unique perspective may be different from what people are used to, but it pays off in the long run. If leaders don't want to miss any opportunities for success and want to keep pace with fast-changing business environments, they should craft diverse teams with people who all bring their different perspectives, personalities, and unique values to the table. Let's start finding value in the difference instead of finding comfort in conformity.

Reason 4: Engaged employees unleash their potential

Frederic Laloux describes another trend in his book *Reinventing Organizations*[12]. Organizations are transforming from command-and-control hierarchies to self-organizing networks of autonomous people. The purpose of this transformation within modern organizations is to acknowledge the unique value and problem-solving ability of all employees. When strengths are acknowledged, people seem to excel without a restricting hierarchic structure as long as they have strong autonomy and are led by a purpose instead of their desire to fit in.

Research performed by Gallup[13] has found that people who use their strengths every day are six times more likely to be engaged on the job. Despite the fact that, for a long time, learning and development focused on improving weak competencies, we now realize that if we focus on strengths, there is more room for growth.

I remember facilitating a training on creative thinking for a group of senior employees of a steel company in the Netherlands. The first morning, one of them, Pete, came in saying, "I'll survive the day!" while waving a little puzzle book at his colleagues. He wasn't

---

[12] Frederic Laloux, *Reinventing Organizations* (Nelson Parker, 2014)

[13] Peter Flade, Jim Asplund, and Gwen Elliot, "Employees Who Use Their Strengths Outperform Those Who Don't," *Gallup Business Journal* (2015)

interested in creative thinking at all. In all his one-on-one sessions, he had received feedback that he was failing to stretch his thinking. He wasn't able to keep up with the organization's demands and was therefore turning into a sarcastic, grumpy old man.

Unfortunately, he wasn't the only one who displayed a sarcastic attitude. Our original setup for the day definitely wouldn't work, so we decided to start with identifying each individual's unique value to the company. An edge of Pete's initial sarcasm faded. Later, we decided to introduce some challenging manufacturing issues for the group to solve.

Pete's unique value to his team was his immense manufacturing knowledge and his willingness to bring that knowledge to the table, which, when introduced at the right time, is an important part of the creative process. Multiple teams asked him to share bits of his knowledge. Pete transformed from being a sarcastic, closed-off man into a vital, enthusiastic, and, above all, engaged, expert. When the training finished, we saw Pete in the lobby waiting with his wife, who had come to pick him up. His eyes glowed with pride when he introduced us to her. People just start to radiate when their unique value is acknowledged and used in the right moment.

There are several ways to identify the strengths of employees. A popular method within the learning and development industry is the StrengthsFinder Assessment, which is so much better than merely focusing on a long list of competencies. But is it possible to capture your unique value in standardized tests? To a certain extent, I think they show in which direction you have to search. My main concern is that those tests don't make a distinction between skills that are true to you and make you stand out, and the skills that you developed to conform and fit in. If you're looking to unleash unused human potential within your organization or are looking for the autonomous, engaged, and creative sides of your employees, you would be better to focus on the authentic root of the skills. Learn more about this in Part II of this book: *Standing Out*. But first, we are about to dive into Part I: *Fitting In,* to discover what makes us hide our autonomous, engaged, and creative sides in situations when it really matters.

"We hide certain aspects and adjust ourselves, comparing ourselves to others and trying to match them, competing to become people *other than who we really are.*"

PART I
FITTING IN

One day, in one of our sessions, Cara described how she had become someone she was not—how she had crafted this ideal person to strive towards.

> There was a perfect ideal to which I had subscribed, and I was doing my utmost to become it. I wanted to be admired and "at the top of my game," and I felt the only way to do that was to stamp out those areas that did not confirm to the ideal—my imperfections.

However, after a while, she started to realize how stamping out authentic areas had made her into someone she could hardly recognize. She realized her imperfections actually complemented her and slowly started to accept that it was okay to be herself, her whole self.

I, too, had vulnerabilities and imperfections, and decided I should embrace them and remove that dreadful pressure of the inauthenticity of trying to be someone I am not. The disappointment of "this is not who I am or will become" was at first huge—I had been so invested in "becoming" and being perfect. But I am slowly accepting that it is okay to be me.

Yes, it really is okay to be you. In fact, we like others who are authentic and who don't try to be perfect. But that unattainable perfection is still something most of us strive for. We hide certain aspects and adjust ourselves, comparing ourselves to others and trying to match them, competing to become people other than who we really are. We try so hard to become successful that we pretend, smile, and agree, even when we honestly feel otherwise. We are constantly seduced to conform to a certain ideal, blending in, in order to belong.

Like sailors learning how to handle headwinds in order to reach their final destiny, understanding our tendencies to fit in is an essential first step to developing our abilities to stand out. This part of the book introduces everything there is to know about fitting in: Why do we fit in, what are the benefits of being very good at it, and what exactly do we sacrifice by fitting in? And how do we free ourselves from these tendencies?

Will you ignore
your own feelings
and needs
in order to fit in
and meet all
the expectations
around you?

TWO — WHY DO WE WANT TO FIT IN?

Do you know the Matryoshka dolls, also known as Russian nesting dolls? They are a set of wooden dolls of increasing size, often beautifully painted, placed one inside another. I often use these dolls as a metaphor for our personal development. The different dolls stand for the different (unconscious) reasons we fit in and cover ourselves, as if we have a different skin. We start off with the tiny doll, pure and authentic. Then, because of our biological wiring, we change who we are in order to "stay safe," the second doll. Our culture influences to alter our authentic core with another cover of social norms to fit in with the rest, the third doll. Then, there are circumstances in life and work that influence our behaviors and attitudes in a psychological way, the fourth doll, until there's a point where we have so many different covers, we don't remember who was originally inside, deep down. Therefore, it's wise to become aware of the several ways we cover ourselves in order to discover which ones are authentic and which aren't.

The biological reasons why we fit in

You might not realize it while doing so, but we're actually biologically wired to adapt to a group's standards in order to survive. Wanting to fit in is a built-in tendency for most human beings.

We are wired to conform

The book *Man the Hunted*[14] describes how we are wired to survive and preserve our species, and how that makes us more inclined to conform. For an enormous amount of time, humans depended on being part of a group. Groups were a means to defend against possible attacks from a large predator, whether by alerting others or by joining forces to fight and protect. As a species, we became social and lived near one another because it was much safer.

You and I, and I would say almost every other human being, conform rather than stand out, because the threat of being separated from the group, being abandoned, and standing outside of that group was—and still is—just too risky according to our evolutionary biological system. It used to lead to separation and exclusion, which led to death.[15]

This wiring still has an enormous impact on us despite the fact that we aren't prey for large predators anymore. When we are about to do something that makes us stand out, like entering a stage with hundreds of eyes staring at us, our body reacts automatically. The fear of being abandoned is still ingrained in our system and makes us think twice of doing something that involves the risk of being rejected.

You might have heard about the fight, freeze, or flight mechanism, introduced in the early twentieth century by physiologist Walter Bradford Cannon. Either we start fighting or start fleeing when we are in acute danger, or even when we assume we are in danger. Whether we fight, freeze, or take flight depends on how we have

---

[14] Donna Hart and Robert Wald Sussman, *Man the Hunted: Primates, Predators, and Human Evolution* (Basic Books, 2005).

[15] Glenn Croston, *The Real Story of Risk* (Prometheus Books, 2012).

learned to deal with threat, as well as the innate fight or flight "program" built into our brain.

Do you ever think about what is happening inside your body when you are about to do something outside of your comfort zone? It all starts with our hypothalamus, a region in the forebrain that sends an emergency message to our autonomic nervous system, which sets in motion several bodily reactions. Our body starts producing hormones like adrenaline and cortisol and a cascade of events is initiated. Our heart, breath, pupils, and organs change in order to deal with threatening dangers. All of this happens beyond your control inside your body in just a few seconds.

I don't know about you, but I find it challenging to ignore my red cheeks and rapid breath when I am on the verge of asking a risky question in a room full of experts. Or to not notice my rising heartbeats and trembling voice when I am about to confront someone. It seems so much easier just to be "normal" and not to be in the spotlight, right? Our body helps us conform and avoid situations that may cause these uncomfortable reactions and feelings. Our brains just prefer to follow the crowd.

The difference between women and men

Generally speaking, men and women fit in differently. When confronted with stress, many women choose self-sacrifice over confrontation, so they can rescue the relationship and avoid conflict. A woman often lets other people's needs determine her limits while her own needs are ignored, while men let challenge and competition set the pace and are usually led by their rivals' efforts or their employers' agendas.

The main biological reason that men and women react differently to stress is the release of three hormones: cortisol, epinephrine, and oxytocin. Cortisol and epinephrine raise a person's blood pressure and increase the circulating blood sugar level. But the hormone oxytocin makes the difference in this case. In a female body, when cortisol and epinephrine rush through the bloodstream in a stressful situation, oxytocin gets released from the brain and provokes nurturing and relaxing emotions. A male body releases oxytocin as well, but in much smaller amounts[16]. So, the next time you are in a tense situation, realize that you and your colleagues' hormones affect the emotional reflexes in different ways. Women are more likely to adjust to save relationships due to the oxytocin. Men are more likely to feel a tendency to compete because of the cortisol and epinephrine.

How we are encouraged to fit in culturally

Don't underestimate the ways in which we are influenced by our culture and society. It's interesting to see how our culture and society shape our brains to think it's better to conform to a certain ideal image than to go off the beaten path and stand out in your own original way.

The rise of "being liked" in the twentieth century

Pioneer in cultural history Warren Susman[17] appointed the transition from the nineteenth into the twentieth century as a shift from Character Culture to Personality Culture. Whereas the older culture valued morality and discipline, the newer culture emphasized being

---

[16] Shelley, Taylor, Laura Cousino Klein, Brian Lewis a.o "Biobehavioral Responses to Stress in Females: Tend-and-Befriend, not Fight-or-Flight," *Psychological Review* (2000, Vol 107, No. 3, 411-429)

[17] Warren Susman, *Culture as History: Transformation of American Society in the Twentieth Century* (Smithsonian Institution Press, 2003)

WHY DO WE WANT TO FIT IN? 31

liked and admired as more favorable. In the twentieth century, an increasing dominance of "personality" entered the American culture. The idea of having a good personality wasn't a thing until the twentieth century. The idea of fitting in became a serious goal. From then on, we have been programmed to desire new products to fulfill our lives.

Paul Mazur, a Wall Street banker for Lehman Brothers in the 1930s, wrote[18]:

> We must shift America from a needs, to a desires culture. People must be trained to desire, to want new things even before the old had been entirely consumed. We must shape a new mentality in America. Man's desires must overshadow his needs.

In order to create a market for certain items, clever businesses would advertise products in careful language, designed to influence potential buyers into seeing the necessity of owning particular products.[19]

The display of perfect and ideal images of how we should look or behave started to arise. Portraits of the seemingly perfect house, perfect relationship, perfect family, perfect body, perfect holiday, made us want those things because we equate having them with happiness and not having them with unhappiness—advertising campaigns, like that of Serentil, a tranquilizer, dove into people's anxiety, using payoffs like, "For the anxiety that comes from not fitting in." Our consumer culture thrives on our desire to fit in and repeats that message

---

[18] Gus Lubin, "There's A Staggering Conspiracy Behind The Rise Of Consumer Culture" *Business Insider* (2013)

[19] Maryland State Archives, *The Rise of Advertisement and American Consumer Culture,* http://teaching.msa.maryland.gov

again and again: *Your life will be great if you are the same as these wonderful, happy people.*

Mental models

All the examples and images we see, hear, and learn all day at school or work, and even at rest or play, shape our mental models. These mental models are like boxes in which we immediately place a message that comes into our brain to help us sift through and process huge amounts of input to prevent us from becoming overwhelmed. Each time a message is presented, it creates neurological pathways like ruts and grooves in your brain and automatic neural networks are built. For example, if we constantly hear and see that the color pink is associated with girls, we start to associate pink with girls. But why exactly is this color girlish? Why not yellow, blue, or purple?

Imagine what mental models are created each moment that make you want to fit in. The whole day, we are surrounded by mental models in advertising and media that suggest what we should love, where we should live, how we should dress, and what we should buy in order to fit in. We hardly realize that these perfect pictures offer an imperfect representation of reality. The people are not exposed as real human beings, having both outstanding qualities as flaws like the rest of us. So we seem to chase an unreachable ideal. In our attempt to be as beautiful as supermodels and celebrities, we diet and workout. Don't get me wrong. Everyone is entitled to do whatever they want with their bodies, but is our desire to fit a certain image realistic? Aren't we spending a lot of money and attention chasing after unachievable goals?

Role models are carving mental models that may lead to unconscious biases

According to the writers of the book *Heroes*,[20] we are deeply influenced by the mental models of heroes. From a young age, we are exposed to action heroes like Batman, Superman, Spiderman, Iron Man and many more. When you ask the average four-year-old boy what he wants to become, I bet he'll answer firefighter, policeman, or another kind of hero. Heroes and role models tap into basic human needs for survival, like security, happiness, or health. We use these models and attributes in stories because they teach us moral ideas. They have qualities that we wish for ourselves—we need ideals to strive for and to guide us forward.

However, if we are exposed to a specific set of role models, like action heroes, mental models get carved into our brains. If these heroes are all muscled, we automatically equate muscles with heroism. If these heroes never cry, we (especially their fans, young boys) might get the message that it's not cool to express sad emotions. These role models can carve unconscious biases from an early age onwards. Think of our automatic association between leadership and masculinity. We often do not realize mental models are shaped when our kids constantly are exposed to male heroes in TV shows, movies, and books.

The "think manager-think male" phenomenon psychologist Virginia Schein introduced in the 1970s is still alive in our unconscious bias. Despite a lot of research that proves differently, our unconscious bias defines a successful leader as assertive, dominant, and decisive, which are all skills we attach to males. In fact, when a woman is assertive, she is often called bitchy. When she is decisive, she is called

---

[20] Scott T. Allison and George R. Goethals, *Heroes: What They Do and Why We Need Them* (Oxford University Press, 2010)

pushy. It's no surprise that women are struggling with this "double bind" and with their urge to fit in when it comes to leadership.

Fortunately, our society is slowly becoming aware of these unconscious biases and is beginning to use a variety of role models to promote inclusion. The hero in the new online game *Zero Dawn*, Aloy, is a girl. Or famous athletes, like NBA player Jason Collins, who became the first openly gay man to play in one of the four major North American sports.

An overflow of "recipes" teaches us to stop thinking autonomously

My son loves to cook. Several Saturday mornings, we wake up with the most delicious smells coming from the kitchen. At first, I encouraged him to use recipes since his pies were, let's say, very original and very different from what you would find in the bakery. But thinking about it, I started to admire him because of his refusal to follow other people's recipes and let him just go for it. He is already following step-by-step how-to rules every day at school. I understand that we have to learn the system first in order to play with it, but in some cases I think our current society might be more involved in the perfect end-result than imagination and play.

Even Lego sets use step-by-step instructions nowadays. What does that teach us? To follow orders really well? To be awesome at thinking *inside* the box? Professor Gundersen Engeset and her colleague Dr. Page Moreau found that following standard instructions on Lego sets would reduce creativity in solving future problems.[21] Isn't this exactly the opposite of what Lego's mission was about?

---

[21] C. Page Moreau and Marit Gundersen Engeset, "The Downstream Consequences of Problem-Solving Mindsets: How Playing with Legos Influences Creativity" in *American Marketing Association Journal of Marketing Research* (2015).

To be able to solve global complex issues, we might want to teach our kids and ourselves to unleash our imagination and to deliver original, amazing results that might not (yet) look perfect, but definitely help us to build our creative confidence.

Social media increases our tendency to compare

We live in a society where showing "everything is fine!" is our default, and we support that by using social media. We can constantly see everyone's highlights in their timeline, which can make us doubt our own lives and feelings of belonging. When I see Facebook posts by friends in their finest outfits having fun with other friends on a Friday night, I catch myself wondering why I'm not out having fun like that. Of course, it's my choice to stay home and relax, but I still second-guess myself by comparing my life to my friends.

Using social media, we constantly have to keep in mind that we only get to see a snapshot instead of the whole story. When I post pictures of my kids having fun at the beach, you are not able to see the not-so fun times like how one of them refused to leave the house that morning. I remember a scene at a restaurant in Shanghai where the context was completely different from the actual picture. A group of four beautiful young women sat at the table. They were barely speaking. They were all in their own world staring at their phones, until one of them asked the waiter to take a picture.

Suddenly, the whole atmosphere changed: they laughed with arms around each other, having fun. They were showing their social followers that they had a fun night, while hiding the fact that their reality was completely different and actually quite saddening. If we don't pay attention, we believe that "their" lives are better, more successful, and more joyful than ours and we change ours accordingly.

As Theodore Roosevelt so aptly said, "Comparison is the thief of joy." When our tendency to fit in is triggered, we start to fill our own social media timeline with successful joyful pictures, and the cycle continues.

We are so attached to winning that vulnerability is not an option

The competitive pull is strong, and maybe even stronger in the US compared with other places in the world. I remember one evening when our American friend shared his life philosophy: "Life is competitive." At the time, my jaw dropped. Could he really think that life is all about winning? But when I moved to the United States a year later, I started seeing how winning and losing are important themes in this competitive society. "Only if we win, we do succeed in life," is an underlying foundation in many lives. The race to make things better, faster, and stronger is apparent in almost everything—education, advertisements, conversations. Nothing wrong with wanting to improve ourselves, right? But this quest for perfectionism goes hand in hand with the illusion that we constantly have to fit in and therefore have to fight our own vulnerability.

In our quest to never lose, we often make unhealthy choices. In the short term, we might think our perfectionism helps to fight our limits, such as athletes who take steroids to endure when their actual muscles need rest or the youth-obsessed who fight nature and wrinkles through procedures and injections. Even picture day forms at school offer a retouching option for whitening eyes and teeth in our kids' photos.

In the long run, these attempts all keep us from being real and feeling satisfied with ourselves. Living in this kind of world, it is not crazy that we flinch when people encourage us to embrace our vulnerability. Why on earth would we do that? We are constantly programmed to link being vulnerable with losing, failing, or being not good enough as we really are.

Different cultures

Without a doubt, our tendency to change ourselves to fit in depends on where we are raised. Hofstede's theory on Cultural Dimensions[22] shows that in individualistic cultures (most Western countries) individual thoughts are encouraged and people have a lower tendency to conform. Uniqueness has a more positive connotation—it means freedom and independence. Whereas collectivist cultures tend to conform more easily because fitting in and conformity have positive connotations of connectedness and harmony in East Asian culture.[23]

This cultural difference is also fed by their differing education systems, which, of course, are founded on the same individualistic or collectivist principles. Education systems in Asian countries are focused on large amounts of knowledge and an appreciation of hierarchy. My Japanese friend could teach me about which paintings Dutch painter Vermeer had painted all his life. I didn't have a clue myself. But she didn't learn how to formulate her own individual opinion. It seems as if she was taught ideas instead of being asked what her own ideas would be.

The Japanese have a saying, "The nail that sticks up gets hammered down." In other words, act like other people and don't show off, or else. Western education systems are more geared towards teaching children to formulate their own opinions, although there are still guidelines and structure for those opinions.

Looking at another level, however, I wouldn't say this difference is surefire, based on my experience living in China and Japan as well as in the US and in Europe. Chinese people hang their underwear out-

---

[22] Geert Hofstede, Gert van Hofstede and Michael Minkov, *Cultures and Organizations: Intercultural Cooperation and Its Importance for Survival* (McGraw-Hill Education, 2010)

[23] Dr. Charles Stanger and Dr. Rajiv Jhangiani, Dr. Hammond Tarry, *Principles of Social Psychology - 1st International Edition* (Open Textbook Project, 2014)

side without impropriety, and parks are full of people who dance, perform, lie in the sun, and do their thing without any form of shame. I wonder what people here in the United States would say if I would dance "like nobody is watching" in the park. Also, my hairstylist told me how other mothers, while waiting to pick up their children, would ask her, "What church do you go to?" The peer pressure almost made her make up a fake answer, despite her being a Buddhist.

Each culture has its own ideas on what is "unacceptable." One sure thing is that our culture and social norms have an amplifying effect on our tendency to fit in.

The psychology of fitting in

Next, let's take a look at the field of psychology. We've seen how we are biologically wired to fit in and how our culture encourages us to do so even more. What does psychology teach us? Our tendency to conform is shown in a lot of astonishing experiments performed by psychological researchers. One of them is described next. After that, it is time to dig a little deeper into what is happening in our minds and how our behaviors are shaped accordingly.

We conform to what the majority says, even when it seems different

Numerous psychological experiments show that we conform as human beings. You might have heard about the Asch Line Study. I remember hearing about it in university and still think it is kind of astonishing. Asch invited 50 male participants for a vision test. In a group setting, the participants were asked questions about the length of lines. Only one person within the room was a real participant, the other were part of the experiment and were explicitly asked to give the wrong answer. Would the participant conform to their wrong answers or stick with his own truth? On average, about one-third of the participants who were placed in this situation went along and conformed with the clearly incorrect majority on the critical trials. In the control group, with no pressure to conform to confederates, less than one percent of participants gave the wrong answer.

Why do people give the wrong answer when they know it's not right? In the interview afterwards, most of them said that they did not really believe their conforming answers, but they had gone along with the group for fear of being ridiculed or thought "peculiar."[24]

I understand that you will not always say "A" just because everyone else in the meeting says "A" if you really think it's "B." But don't underestimate the sometimes-unconscious power of group thinking. When we work in groups, this psychological phenomenon is likely to occur.[25] Our desire for harmony and conformity leads to a decrease of our mental efficiency, reality testing, and moral judgment. You may have avoided raising a controversial issue. You may have stopped yourself from providing alternative solutions in groups that didn't seem open to it. *What would have happened if you had not refrained from adding the controversy?*

We defend our core

Let's now take a look on a deeper level. Why do we change our behaviors in order to fit in? What happens when we do that? A simple model to represent a human being is a circle with a center in the

---

[24] Saul McLeod "What is Conformity?", *Simply Psychology* (2016)

[25] Irving L. Janis, *Victims of Groupthink* (Houghton Mifflin, 1972)

middle. The plus in the center is surrounded by minuses (J. de Dreu).[26]

The plus resembles your essence: you, in the purest form. It is who you essentially are, and when you act from this core, you stand out—then you are the most authentic you'll ever be.

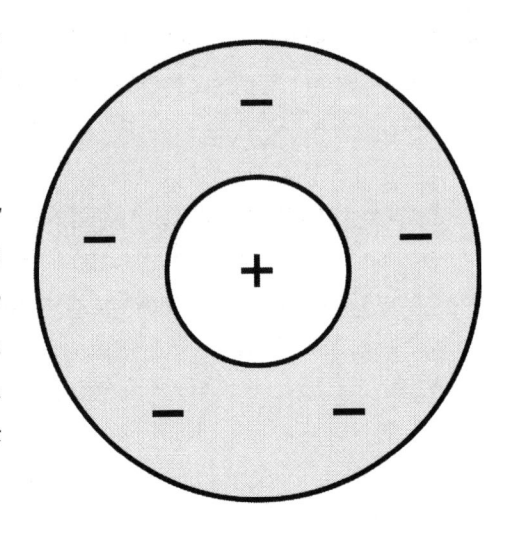

Because this core represents 100 percent "you," imagine how you feel if that part is affected. Your reason of being is affected. That hurts. Fortunately, this core is extremely well protected. Thank you, Mother Nature! The vulnerability of this core is cared for by the minuses.

The minuses are your defense mechanisms. To deal with conflict and problems in life, Sigmund Freud stated that the ego employs a range of defense mechanisms. Protective mechanisms operate at an unconscious level and help ward off unpleasant feelings such as anxiety or shame.

Think of the last time you received criticism about your work. (Or do you make sure you'll never get criticism?) How did you react? Maybe you blushed and made excuses, or maybe you got angry and decided to work harder next time. Or were you just stunned and didn't know how to react? We all have our own ways of dealing with uncomfortable situations. Just like we all have unique Talents, we also

---

26 Jan de Dreu, *Leef: acht opwekkende aanwijzingen* (Schouten & Nelissen, 2013)

have unique defense mechanisms. All of these mechanisms were built in our past, and they were created to help us "survive" as children and teenagers.

Let me explain. As young children, we are totally open. Imagine a baby or toddler. They have no social defense mechanisms in place. A young human being is 100 percent authentic. They are not concerned with taking care of other people's feelings and are not busy interpreting other people's actions. This young child is receiving everything with a completely open mind, totally vulnerable and surrendering to life's circumstances. On the flipside, everything that is noticed inside is coming out without any reservation. If they're hungry, they're screaming for food. If they feel happy, they laugh and smile. And if they're in pain, you'll hear that! If they are excited about seeing a bird or a car or a shiny rock, they'll let their mommy or daddy know that too.

Children are the best at expressing themselves without holding back. Unfortunately, the way they express themselves doesn't always fit their context. When their brains develop to the point that they become able to label others' behaviors, they start holding back, because what they express is not always convenient. Their brains aren't yet developed in such a way that they know how to tune in with their environment following the social norms. So their enthusiasm is not always welcomed, and in some sad cases, their existence will be denied by neglect. They will stop expressing themselves. They will start paying attention to the reactions around them.

You might remember a remark or an event in your childhood that made you decide, *oh, I might have to tone it down or I'll just keep this for myself.* At a certain point in our childhood, we start to reckon with the outside world. We start using cues to learn how to fit in and escape judging. It's in our youth that we start adding filters to how we experience the world and how we express ourselves. We all develop certain ways to react to our surroundings without being aware of it.

The book *Drama of the Gifted Child* [27] by Alice Miller wonderfully describes this pattern towards fitting in. Every one of us chose a unique way of dealing with situations in our upbringing. But children who are gifted with a high dose of sensitivity will attune to their parents' moods. They will ignore their own feelings and needs in order to fit in and meet all the expectations around them. They choose not to be burdens, to blend in and to try to be perfect. They are sensitive to the emotional needs of their parents and will try to take care of their needs.

My client Vera had a mother who was suffering with severe illness. From an early age, she was the actual caretaker in the house since her father couldn't deal with his wife's state of being. Vera made sure her mother took the right medicines at the right time. She never invited friends home because that would be too much of a burden. Vera stopped being a carefree child at the age of only seven years old. She took all the responsibility and became very good at taking care of other people's problems, instead of her own. The drama in all of this is that Vera and other such gifted children did not learn to develop how to listen to their own inward needs because they were constantly focused outward, on others' needs. Their core seems empty because they never acknowledged the existence or importance of their own true self.

---

[27] Alice Miller, *Drama of the Gifted Child: The Search for the True Self* (Basic Books, 1997)

"What's lost inwardly must be gained outwardly" is the title of an episode of Borgen[28], one of my favorite Danish TV series. When we lose "what we essentially are," we are working hard to retrieve our loss in the outside world. We work really hard to get recognition and approval when we feel insecure and inadequate.

How about you? Are you more focused on the needs of others than on your own? When people ask you personal questions—such as *what do you feel?* or *what do you really want in life?*—*do you feel uncomfortable?* If so, you might recognize this drama of the gifted child happening in your own life.

In the following pages, you can read what you gained by your ability to fit in and what you sacrificed. You can learn what you can do to loosen yourself from this burden as you get to know and acknowledge your own true feelings and needs as you finally tap into your greatest strength; stand out and shine.

---

[28] Borgen, *Danish Broadcaster Corporation* (2010)

To make things work,
we want to be considered
"one of them."

THREE — BENEFITS OF FITTING IN AT WORK

You probably know best what there is to gain with fitting in because you might have done it for a long time already. Perhaps it paid off to some extent in the sense that your career is successful. You might have modeled leaders who were successful in their roles. You might have agreed with opinions of important stakeholders in order to be "on the right team" and receive budget for your projects. Also, you might have tweaked yourself to tick boxes in order to be considered for an attractive promotion. Yes, certainly, there are advantages to adapting yourself and changing bits of yourself while working in a company. In fact, in a certain aspect, blending in with others pays off, and here is why.

High-sensitivity makes things run smoothly

During my Master's in Innovation Management, most assignments consisted of teamwork. In assigned groups, we had to design products and services for specific target groups. These processes contained a massive amount of discussions and decisions that led to conflicts in some of the groups. Somehow, I never experienced much trouble in my groups. We worked diligently until we reached our design solutions. Yes, we had discussions, but everything was always very peaceful in contrast to my friend's groups. Somehow, it seemed she always ended up in groups where conflicts reigned. Sometimes conflicts led to better results, sometimes they ran amok, but my friend always ended up exhausted by the tense group dynamics.

Aside from the fact that I might have been lucky with the composition of the teams where I ended up, I think my fitting-in abilities also played an important role. I was making sure things ran smoothly. I chose not throw a wrench into things despite the fact that I might have had another opinion. I wanted to keep things harmonious.

We 'fitting-inners' have a highly developed sensitivity for how things work in the room. This sensitivity enables us to iron out disharmonies before they turn into conflicts, which sometimes is incredibly constructive.

Fitting in improves communication and integration

Have you ever heard of mirroring? We all do it. When someone you're talking to leans back, you might find yourself automatically leaning back as well. I find myself doing that quite often, and it makes me laugh inside. Besides the fact that it's funny, it's actually effective. Mirroring others will leave the other with positive feelings and can make us more persuasive.[29] It's called limbic synchrony, and it's hardwired into the human brain. In our tendencies to fit in, we subconsciously switch our body postures to match those of the other person, which signals that we are connected and engaged. It's a proven method to build rapport or to increase a person's comfort when they are resistant.

Cultural fit increases success

Fitting in helps us to connect with the people around us and with our companies' cultures. In our attempts to fit in, we adhere to the subtle customs and belief systems. In case we are sensitive, and I be-

---

[29] Jeff Thompson, "Mimicry and Mirroring Can Be Good ... or Bad", *Psychology Today* (2012)

lieve in essence we all are, we spot every sign that tells us what's successful and what isn't. We adjust our communication styles, our attitudes and even our wardrobes to feel a part of the culture of the company we are working for.

A 2005 meta-analysis by Kristof-Brown[30] reports that employees who fit in well with their coworkers and supervisor had greater job satisfaction and were more likely to remain within their organization. It makes sense. To make things work, we want to be considered "one of them." If we go with the flow and swim in the same direction, we have the highest chance of arriving where the company wants us to go.

Attuning yourself to what is needed increases your chances for promotions

It pays to know how to play the game and to be sensitive to what the situation asks for. If you are a chameleon and are very good at blending in, you probably possess a variety of different skills and have learned when to use them. Countless studies show that women are behind on the leadership ladder, but one important study by Stanford University shows that women who have learned to master their ability to fit in to their advantage have better chances of success. Women who know when to switch male traits on and off (aggression, assertion, and confidence) get more promotions than men and other women.[31]

---

[30] Amy L Kristof-Brown, Ryan D Zimmerman, and Erin C Johnson, "Consequences of Individuals' Fit at Work: Meta-analysis of Person-Job, Person-Organization, Person-Group and Person-Supervisor Fit," *Personnel Psychology*, (2005; 58, 2)

[31] Marguerite Rigoglioso, "Researchers: How Women Can Succeed in the Workplace" *Insights by Stanford Business* (2011)

Employees who fit in make hierarchic systems run smoother

Traditional hierarchical organizations, controlled primarily from the top, benefit from people who are more likely to follow than to question decisions. The military is a classic example of a hierarchical organizational structure. Power and responsibility are clearly specified and allocated to individuals according to their standing or position in the hierarchy.

In a hierarchy, authority, responsibility, and job functions are clearly defined along with the road to promotions. For things to run smoothly, standards need to be defined. Here, people who are high achievers, excellent at executing orders, and running businesses as expected are rewarded more often than people who disrupt the systems.

Fitting in helps us to feel a sense of belonging

Having moved from my home in the Netherlands to two different continents (Asia and North America), I can say that my ability to fit in certainly paid off in settling in. I found friends and connected easily by blending in. My sensitivity for dos and don'ts helped me get along with people. I still find myself bowing slightly as a sign of respect when answering a Japanese person. In the US, I find myself asking personal questions to strangers that wouldn't be appropriate in Asia or Europe. Overall, I think our ability to fit in helps us make new connections faster—it makes us feel not so strange.

Overall, the ability to fit in is wonderful and I am grateful for our ability to blend in every now and then. Without it, our species probably would be extinct and many more disharmonies would occur. Our ability to fit in brought us far in life. It served us to survive in a world full of insecurities. Challenges arise when we start to change ourselves in order to fit in in such a way that we lose our authenticity, when we trade and sometimes completely forget about our valuable qualities in order to belong.

"If you force everyone in some sort of a cookie-cutter mold, you lose a lot of channels where they could add value from their uniqueness and the way they think about the world."

- Maureen Hughes

FOUR — SACRIFICES OF FITTING IN AT WORK

Francesca Gino, professor at Harvard Business School, performed intensive research[32] among 2,097 US employees about the effects of conformation. Her research shows that conforming takes a heavy toll on both individuals and enterprises. Employees who felt a need to conform reported a less positive work experience on several dimensions than did other employees. Her research shows that organizations consciously or unconsciously urge employees to leave their real selves at home. Both employees and their organizations pay a price: decreased engagement and productivity, and less innovation. These results are interesting food for thought for your organization.

Now, let's zoom in on what toll fitting in and conformity take on you.

While fitting in, we fade away

Maureen Hughes, global partner in Consumer Business at Deloitte, was one of the first female partners in consulting and experienced multiple times when she had to behave more like a man to be successful. Later on she realized that too much fitting in took its toll. "I always felt I was fighting for the right to be there. I was fighting to survive, and that takes an awful amount of energy." She realized that however hard she tried, she could never be one of the boys. All she

---

[32] Francesca Gino, "Let your workers rebel" *Harvard Business Review* (2016)

could become was the poorest version of one of the boys. "So if that is the case, I might as well try less hard and be more myself and see where that leads me."

In Maureen's case, it led to success and her being a role model for many people in her organization. Currently, she is an advocate for everyone who is perceived as an outlier. "If you force everyone in some sort of a cookie-cutter mold, you lose a lot of channels where they could add value from their uniqueness and the way they think about the world."

If we grow up with a strong tendency to fit in, our muscle to attune ourselves to the expectations of others is extremely developed. We do whatever we need to in order to fulfill other people's needs and to avoid conflicts. We try to please others and look for their approval. In becoming that "perfect" person, we lose something very precious. We lose ourselves. We shrivel from the inside. Our insides evaporate in such a sense that they even feel hollow. It feels as if we don't have any foundation to lean on.

Somehow, a limiting belief—that we have to trade our authenticity for approval—was planted in our minds. We think we have to behave *the same* as others in order to fit in. Brené Brown[33] writes: "Many of us suffer from this split between who we are and who we present to the world in order to be accepted. But we're not letting ourselves be known, and this kind of incongruent living is soul-sucking." In our quest to belong, we think being ourselves isn't allowed.

I remember my conversations with Sammy, who came to me because she did not feel confident. She undervalued everything she did. In our first conversations, she shared how she looked up to others

---

[33] Brené Brown, "Life Lessons: Brené Brown On Shame, Courage, And Vulnerability" Huffington Post (2015)

and how she was busy pleasing them by working hard. She was so busy copying how others added value that she didn't have an inkling what her own unique value was. In excelling in catching other people's signals, Sammy completely ignored her own sense of self. Her muscle to attune herself to her own needs, desires, and qualities was underdeveloped.

I can understand how she became so insecure, because her foundation was never developed. She didn't know *what* could make her confident. All her attempts at hiding her insecurities and appearing strong actually made her lose much of her strength. I estimate she was only using 25 percent of her potential. Imagine what effect this loss of potential had on herself and her workplace?

We sacrifice our health

As I've already mentioned in this book, I was a total pro in observing what other people in the room might feel. I was easy to communicate with, never the subject of conflicts, received a lot of compliments, and was successful in my work. I made sure my own feelings and emotions went underground and hid in a shelter. No one else, including myself, was allowed to look those feelings in the eye. It was more desirable to act like the energized superwoman who was up for anything than to be my true self who sometimes had to drag herself to work. It was too painful to realize I was actually exhausted by my need to fulfill everyone's needs. Besides that, when there was a conflict at the office, I chose to ignore it, but then the issues became bigger and bigger.

That is, until a certain point. Stress levels started to grow behind my everlasting smile. I had many colds, and I started hyperventilating. Finally, it was the amazing rescue system within my body that made me look in the mirror and forced me to see my actual situation.

I had ruined my immune system by ignoring my own needs for a very long time.

By becoming pros at fitting in, we are creating very high and unrealistic expectations for ourselves, and we have to work really hard to meet those so we don't disappoint others and ourselves. Meeting all of the demands of our 24-hour connected world is hard work. Constantly striving for peak performance creates stress. It's usually not a problem when stressful moments are alternated with moments of relaxation; but in today's society, our stress levels are usually constantly on high. Who hasn't checked their emails right before falling asleep and again just after waking up, even before getting into the shower? When we experience chronic stress, our hormones don't give up on us. They help us to stay in a constant state of alertness or hyper-arousal. These stress hormones keep overriding other body functions and our immune system gets affected, think about fatigue, weight gain, moodiness, anxiety, thyroid imbalance, and irritability.

By being afraid of difficult emotions, we sacrifice happiness

In our attempt to ignore personal feelings and emotions to appear on our private stage, we also uninvited happiness to appear. "In our attempts to close our hearts to keep peace, we rise a hidden war inside ourselves," writes Michael Derkse.[34] Our society has been very good at numbing these uncomfortable feelings by working hard, smartphones, drugs or other distracting entertainment. Stand-up comedian, Louis C.K., explains why we tend to avoid these sad emotions and other uncomfortable feelings and why we keep on filling our moments with distractions: "When we don't fill our moments, and just sit, a moment of sadness (or anger, or frustration) can hit us.

---

34 Michael Derkse, *De Weg ligt onder de je Voeten: Over het Lef om te Leven*, (Ten Have, 2011)

For a brief moment, we see the reality in all her truth. And that hurts." But he also says, "If we endure those moments, give it our attention, pure joy awaits. If we dare to be vulnerable, we also can experience pure bliss."[35]

He is right*. If we don't allow the painful truth, we don't allow the blissful truth. If we shut ourselves out from feeling sad, we shut ourselves out from feeling happy. I know this might sound discouraging, but if we can endure the difficult moments, it's worth it.

I've met a lot of people in training programs who realized they turned more rational than they were before. For them, dealing with feelings and emotions felt like an unwanted distraction in contexts ruled by efficiency and competition. If a crack of emotions opened up, their autopilots ignored it by just working a little bit harder.

I remember Tom, a participant in one of the leadership training programs I facilitated. He was easygoing and funny. He smoothly executed the first communication exercises with his charm and humor, until we went a level deeper and the trainer actors introduced some confrontations. A sense of surliness replaced his smoothness. I guess the group felt his passive aggressiveness, because they all confronted him with his surliness. He did not know how to answer until he waved away the feedback with jokes.

His humor obviously had been his survival strategy all along. This probably hid a well of undiscovered emotions inside of him, but I decided to wait to ask him about it until the right time came. The following exercise, he casually shared that he had spent his teenager years in a boarding school. When I repeatedly asked him how he felt about it, he brushed his emotions away by saying, "It was a fun time.

---

[35] "Louis CK being alone with emotions," YouTube (2013)

* I doubt if he has been able to fully implement his wisdom in his own life given the accusations of sexual assault in 2017.

I just was a very difficult boy for my parents!" He expressed these words with a smile, but his whole body expressed another set of emotions.

That night at the bar, he approached me and wanted to talk about the fact that he was single. After trying several relationships, he was nearly about to give up. I asked him to tell me about the moment when casual dates changed into relationships, the point where you really start to get to know each other. He admitted that almost all the women accused him of turning into a robotic state when things got difficult. He recognized the fact that he buried himself with work—he would rather feel busy than feel overwhelming emotions. So as soon as any emotions would enter the stage, he either deflected with humor or else he short-circuited, overloaded himself with work, and became the ultimate autopilot. Needless to say, it's no fun to be in a relationship with an unemotional robot. We talked about how his damaged relationship with his parents still stood in the way of all his other connections.

During the rest of the training, he focused on acknowledging his true emotions one step at a time. He became one of my most ambitious participants, and I have to say, this process had the most wonderful outcome. A year and a half later, I received an email that he had proposed to his girlfriend the night before on their trip to Nepal. For the past one and a half years he had been able to switch off his autopilot and dive deep by allowing himself to feel vulnerable emotions and be open. In allowing all existing emotions, he finally felt alive.

We sacrifice important leadership skills

We sacrifice our ability to connect

Like Tom's example explains, as long as we keep our real selves out of the equation, no genuine connection is possible. If we wear masks to hide our true selves, our connections stay on a superficial level. Our masks don't allow a deeper and more meaningful connection. When we connect on a deeper level, we allow the other person to see the real deal, our human side. And yes, it feels risky, vulnerable, and intimate.

Successful finance consultant Anna explained to me how she recently found out that the risk of hiding herself was larger than the risk of showing herself. Allowing herself to be authentic not only improved her relationship with her children, but it allowed her to lead more effectively at work. At a certain leadership level, it's all about trust. Her company allowed her to make impactful decisions only because they trusted her. They trusted her because she had a proven track record, but she noticed from the moment she dared to let her guard down that the level of trust increased enormously and deepened her connections.

We don't trust people who hide parts of themselves or whose words are not congruent with what they show. Our unconsciousness starts to question things, and as a result, we put our masks back on as well, protecting us from connecting on a deeper level.

Imagine a trusted, approachable person within your own environment with whom you feel a connection on a deeper level. I bet two things are happening in your relationship. That person lets their guard down and doesn't try to pretend that everything is perfect, and in doing so, you feel more comfortable letting your guard down as well. A relief, isn't it?

We don't tap into our emotional intelligence

Some of us are pleasers, others act tough. But both reactions have a huge impact on our emotional intelligence.

My friend Brittany always used to please her kids, husband, parents, and friends. She always thought that was her way of giving love, until she realized that she didn't do it out of real love for the other person but because she feared that if she didn't always please, she might end up in conflicts. She later started calling it "false love." Wise insight, don't you agree?

Our false love isn't the same as compassion at all. Compassion is genuinely caring about others, which is different from false love or pity. When we are pleasing, we are being over-emotional but not dealing with the real emotions that might be under the table. It's to avoid conflicts; it's not an act of love.

My client Barbara copied the toughness of her colleagues in order to match expectations. It hurt me to see her toughness because in deep down she seemed like an incredibly warm person. She had the feeling she needed to battle her way through life. Life had taught her that it was easier to arm herself than to open up and let herself shine through.

It might be convenient to live like an unemotional robot from time to time, but the reality is we aren't robots. We are human beings. Next to our rational abilities, we bring our emotions and feelings along with us.

Our ability to deal with emotions and feelings has a huge impact on performance. Did you know that 90 percent of all top performers have a high emotional intelligence quotient? Awareness of your emotions and dealing with another person's emotions within the workplace is 58 percent responsible for job performance[36]. When you let your reactive patterns and autopilot take the lead, I hope you realize you risk losing your connection with your emotional intelligence, one of your most valuable tools in work and life. You lose being in touch with your uniqueness and risk being totally cut off from your feelings and emotions. What about the quality of such a life?

We react instead of create

We live and lead reactively if we orient primarily on safety. While unconsciously fitting in, all we do is react to the outside world. We live up to what is defined by others. We hand over our autonomy. We lose touch with our own ideas, with what we think is best for the situation. We do not have the courage to create. Our ability to create is underdeveloped and is not (yet) our primary focus. We might feel the desire to do something great, to fulfill an important purpose and to make a difference, but the risks that come with it are still too big. But what if we oriented ourselves on the power of that purpose and learned how to deal with the inherent fears? What if we had the courage to create? Well ... what if *you* had the courage to create?

---

[36] Travis Bradberry, "Emotional Intelligence - EQ" *Forbes* (2014)

Between stimulus and response, there is a space.

In that space is our power to choose our response.

In our response lies our growth and our freedom.

- ascribed to Victor Frankl

FIVE — LETTING GO OF OUR MASKS TO HIDE OURSELVES

The dance between fitting in and standing out is a delicate one. If only we could consciously choose which one is best to be in the lead. Because when our fitting-in ability is mostly in the lead, we dance towards a life heavily ruled by others. We dance towards a life conformed to the outside world's needs. What about our inside world? What about our authenticity? Are we really wanting to sacrifice these and other important benefits of standing out as we truly are?

This book isn't a call to stop you from fitting in. This book is, rather, an invitation to become aware of your tendencies, so that you can choose whether it's best to choose to go with the tide or whether it's best to bring your authentic self to the table. So that *you* are in the lead, instead of your automatic pilot.

Between stimulus and response, there is a space

What if you want to orient yourself towards being yourself at work, allowing yourself to be creative, emotionally intelligent, more engaged, and more authentic? How do you ignore the automatic pattern that you've been using for so long? How do you extricate yourself from something that is biologically wired in our bodies and ingrained in our society? Seems impossible, right?

Fortunately, it's not. We certainly can make this sustainable change within ourselves, but we have to understand that we can only influence our own part in this process. We cannot change the way we are biologically wired any more than we can stop our society from trying to impact our mental models. The only thing we can influence is our own reaction and behavior to these events. We can influence our reactive behaviors to leave room for our creative behaviors. The quote that has been ascribed to neurologist and psychiatrist Victor Frankl explains it wonderfully: "Between stimulus and response there is a space. In that space is our power to choose our response. In our response lies our growth and our freedom."

To influence this moment between stimulus and response, we have to master our tendencies. It starts with self-research. You'll have to check in with yourself first in order to stand out and make a difference. You've been so busy with copying others or taking care of others for such a long time that you'll need some time to get to know yourself. Why not study yourself with the same curiosity you study the world around you?

If we want to be more authentic and stand out, we can be brave and try our best as hard as we can, but with the first headwind, we tend to crawl back into our safe cave. We are looking for approaches that treat the problem, rather than the symptom. In this book, I carefully selected three approaches that treat the roots of our difficulties with standing out and showing up as ourselves. These approaches have shown the best results in my practice, as well as for hundreds of people in Pulsar Academy training programs.

The approaches, *Limiting Stories, Dragons and Awareness Levels*, have one thing in common—they all focus on that space between stimulus and response—allowing you to take the lead, give your own response and step into that space where you feel free to be yourself, at home and at work.

It involves some retrospective reflection before we can look ahead and stand out. That can seem scary, but believe me, the process of dreading something is harder than actually dealing with it.

When I was seven years old, I remember I broke a glass cup. It was in the early morning and everyone was still asleep, therefore I decided to sweep it under the front doormat so no one would notice. When my mother heard the crackling glass under her feet, she asked who had broken a glass. That whole day I postponed telling her, but at dinner, I finally admitted that it was me. My mother was not mad at all, just worried about why I had had the urge to sweep it under the mat.

Don't we all have the same tendency for our problems and difficult emotions? We prefer to sweep difficulties under the rug so we don't have to deal with them and just go on with our lives. But the fact is, nothing really disappears—it piles up and makes walking on it incredibly inconvenient. As soon as we dare to face the facts and deal with those irritations, we discover it wasn't that scary at all. If we really want to change things in our lives, we'll have to face the fact that our immunity to change is related to our immunity to acknowledging the truth, even if that truth hurts. I hope you'll find the courage to clear out whatever is under your rug and face your issues. You'll travel much lighter afterwards.

Limiting stories: Do you really believe the story you have been telling yourself for so long?

Why do you stay in prison when the door is wide open? – Rumi

I love this quote. It asks us why we are limiting ourselves even when nobody or nothing is restricting us. I remember the moment I suddenly and fully understood how I was creating my own prison. I was driving in my car and was worrying myself to death. I had to choose between facilitating two events that were planned on the same day. One I felt obliged to do, and the other one I really wanted to do. I had been waiting to facilitate the event close to my heart for over a year. But for the one I felt obliged to do, there were a lot of people addressing my sense of responsibility and urging me to make "the right choice." But what was the right choice?

That moment in my car, it struck me. No one is really able to tell me what to do. I could choose the event that held greater meaning for me. I could. I'd have to bear the consequences of disappointment, rejection, and maybe even lose my job for it, but I could. That moment, I realized how I had created my own "prison." I had reduced my freedom, believing that others ruled my actions.

That moment, the limiting story transformed into a liberating one: *I, myself, can choose what I want to do. I can bear the consequences.* For me, this was huge. And you know what? The effect of my clear communication of what I was going to do and why resulted in no rejections at all. Besides some creative ideas on how to solve my absence, dealing with one mildly disappointed colleague was all it took. We create imaginative stories that limit our freedom. Questioning those stories and transforming them into liberating ones creates room for relief and inventiveness.

What is a limiting story? It is your perception of reality, or something you were told that you had no reason to doubt.

Organizational theorist Robert Anthony once said, "If we see ourselves or believe ourselves to be a certain way, we will act in accordance with that belief, whether it is true or not." Past experiences shaped your way of thinking and shaped the way you view yourself related to the world. If your mother always kept herself thin, you might believe that keeping yourself thin is the way to go. If you had a bad experience on stage while you were performing in a high school play, you might believe that being on the stage isn't something for you. If your parents were always bothered with what the neighbors would think, you might believe you shouldn't show any peculiarities and believe that keeping quiet is better.

You started to believe certain things were true. But who says? Who decides which norms are the ones to follow? These beliefs can sabotage your freedom and create a suffocating prison that doesn't allow you to enjoy, be successful, or make your own choices. It stops you from being creative and standing out the way you can.

How to transform a (people pleaser's) limiting story?

As many limiting stories are built in people's minds every day, luckily, a lot of limiting stories are being transformed as well. I will explain this approach by describing Moira and her limiting story. Moira was a pleasant participant in our Talent Development training. She was cheerful, emphatic towards the other participants, and eager to learn. She was smiling every time I saw her. Her manager wanted to promote her to be team leader, but he was not sure if she was up for the job. As she was always being nice to everyone, he was afraid that she couldn't make any tough decisions. Moira was a typical people pleaser—a "yes" woman.

The second morning of our training program, I started the *Limiting Stories* exercise with the question: *What was a specific moment in your memory where you didn't do or choose what you actually wanted?* I asked the participants to close their eyes and to see this specific moment happening before their eyes. When I asked them to feel sensations in their body to expand this exercise from merely the mental level to the physical level as well, I saw Moira shivering and leaning forward, bowing her head. She was making herself smaller and smaller.

After a few other questions, I asked them to write down the story they told themselves to condone their behavior for themselves. What limited them and what were they telling themselves over and over? Seeing these convictions in black and white helps people to own their stories. Reading their own story, they really face the facts. *Okay, so this is what I do ...*

I asked who was willing to share their limiting story. Moira raised her hand, but as soon as she saw other hands raised, she put her hand down. Even in that moment, she was pleasing, making sure others got attention "they deserved." I asked her to share this time. She started telling how *she always had to be there for others—how otherwise, she would not be accepted.* She followed up all her colleagues' questions before she got her own work done and was making sure her parents had everything they deserved. She never forgot a friend's birthday while taking care of her three children and her husband.

I wondered what she had felt during the exercise. She wavered, entering this vulnerable terrain. She still smiled to make sure we weren't too worried about her. "You must be exhausted," I said at some point. Receiving this acknowledgement of her hidden fatigue, she finally broke down in tears. I was happy about her tears because I sincerely believe that allowing those emotions is a very important step in transforming our limiting stories. Remember? Our immunity to change is related to our immunity to acknowledging the truth, even if that truth hurts. All the energy Moira had been using to ignore her feelings of fatigue could not be used to build new land.

After a while I asked her if she believed her limiting story was true. She knew it was not true, but she was not yet ready to totally disagree with it. I asked her if she would give the same advice to her three children: that they only would be accepted if they were doing things for other people. Her eyes widened. "Of course not!" she answered. "They are accepted—no matter what—they don't have to do things to receive love." I wrote that sentence on the flip chart.

I wondered her if she remembered who had planted the seed for this story to grow in her mind. That inquiry resulted in the insight that her father had been emotionally unavailable and the only way to get his attention had been to try really hard at pleasing him, just as she always saw her mother trying to do. After some more inquiring questions, the root of her pleasing behavior emerged. The underlying positive reason she was pleasing her father was that she was yearning for *connection*.

Connection became the foundational element of her new liberating story. How could this transform her behavior in the present challenges? I invited all the participants to join a visualization to reimagine a challenging situation at work. How could they use their new foundational element of the liberating stories? In Moira's case, how could she use her desire to connect in confronting her colleagues? We practiced this new behavior with training actors and Moira learned that this new behavior was easier than she thought, as long as she knew how to stay connected with her colleagues.

Each morning of a day when Moira knew she would face a difficult conversation, she visualized herself confronting that colleague while keeping the connection. She learned how saying "no" did not mean the connection would be gone. The more she practiced her new behavior, the more she allowed her brain to ingrain new behavioral patterns and let old patterns fade away. Nowadays, she has made incredible progress and actually enjoys being a team leader in charge of difficult decisions.

"Dragons" tend to take over: inviting our fitting-in-tendencies to take the backseat

Have you ever fantasized about leaving everything behind and hiding yourself in a Tibetan monastery meditating to become your authentic self? I did. But you know, you would have to stay there eternally because the real world would challenge you once you returned home. I have learned this after returning from several secluded meditation programs. The ultimate place for practice to become less reactive isn't in a training program (although it definitely helps to kick it off). The ultimate place for practice is in real life. Your tendencies are woken up to life at the office while working, while dealing with difficult colleagues, while preparing for challenging presentations. Your tendencies are woken up in real life, at home, while speaking with that dominant friend, while dealing with your kid's tantrum. Real life offers excellent moments to practice and become a pro at mastering your tendencies.

Our reactive tendencies act like dragons

Like I already mentioned, we have two different sides inside of us. One side is pure and authentic and wants to bring nothing but good things into this world. You might have experienced this side of yours after meditating, walking in nature, listening to music, or while being with your loved ones. You let your guard down. Instead of reacting to show a certain image, to prove or to please, it's wondering and creating. When you let this side shine through, you Stand Out! This side is looking to create connections, create ideas, and meaningfully change any situation. This side is wonderful.

So why aren't we constantly working from this state of mind? Besides the fact that our biological fear triggers are turned on by stress, the purest version of ourselves got hurt while growing up. Our initiatives and the way we expressed ourselves when we were young weren't always appreciated. And I am not even talking about traumas here. It could have been unintended innocent remarks from parents, friends, or teachers. We learned how to "behave," and most of the times that was different from our own innate behavior. Disappointment blocked roads towards free expression, and we programmed ourselves not to act from within.

If a child continuously notices that he is too much of a burden for his parents, he gets hurt and he may grow into an attitude of "I don't care." He'll try to stop feeling by rationalizing everything. Another person in the same situation might choose to adjust herself and become very good at not being a burden for others and forget about her own needs. She will protect herself by her pattern of adjusting.

You might remember the simple drawing of a human being I introduced earlier, with the plus inside a circle, surrounded by minuses? When this theory was introduced to me, I was fascinated by its simplicity. We have two sides: one is my authentic core and is protected by the other side, the tendencies. But when our teacher named these tendencies "dragons," I was totally sold. These tendencies act exactly like dragons. They are highly skilled in defending the treasure.

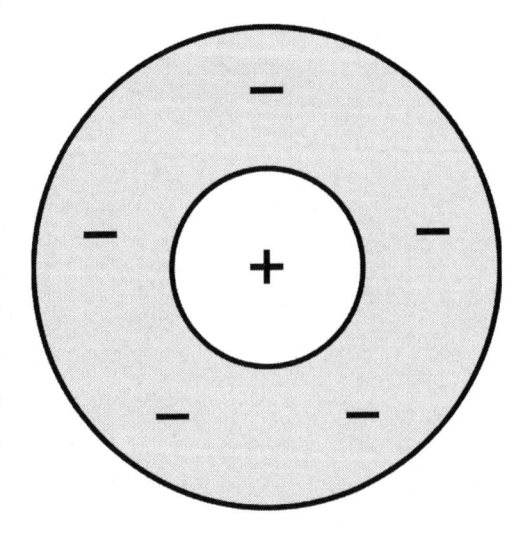

They support us 100 percent with all their good intentions. Also, dragons remind me of childhood stories, and that's where the tendencies start to develop. Dragons are hard to tame, and if you chop off their heads, three-headed monsters arise.

When we are uncomfortable with being ourselves, our dragons awake. One of my most persistent dragons was, and sometimes still is, is my tendency to blend in. Being in stressful situations, challenged to give my own opinion, I am inclined to choose to blend in and withhold my true opinions. And instead of writing "I am inclined to choose to blend in," I should write, "I automatically blended in," because these dragons perform perfectly under unconscious circumstances.

In my coaching practice, I meet many people with dragons that make sure they fit in, like *avoiding confrontations, withdrawing, copying others, pleasing, holding back, thinking negative thoughts, dropping out, striving towards perfectionism, disconnecting, gossiping, giggling, making fun of things.* Also, other dragons emerged, like *patronizing, nagging, whining, being cynical, blocking, procrastinating, knowing better, dominating,* or numbing dragons, like eating, social media browsing, drinking, or *constantly looking for kicks.*

We can be certain of one thing—we all have a full span of dragons driving us to "safer" places. When you visualize all the dragons ruling you and your colleagues in the workplace, you will see an incredibly crowded place. Next time you are in a meeting that doesn't go as planned, try to identify all the dragons that are affecting the meeting. What is your manager's dragon? What's that annoying colleague's dragon? Realize that everyone has different reactive tendencies to defend their vulnerable, authentic core. Become curious about your colleagues' dragons. But most of all, become curious about your own dragons.

What dragon is leading you?

It's interesting to learn which dragon is taking the lead again and again. You will be able to see how it exactly affects you and what it takes to let your authentic core take back the lead. *So, take a moment to reflect and to figure out what your most frustrating dragon might be, following the steps below:*

1. *Make a list* of things you do when you are in uncomfortable situations. What do you see yourself doing or not doing when you try to stand out and be authentic?
   - Write all your tendencies down using verbs, because dragons are not merely emotions or feelings, they make you *do things or take actions* you are fed up with. Dragons either drive you to do things you don't want to, or stop you from doing things you secretly would want to.
   - I encourage you to use your own original words. In many training programs, they limit you with the eight patterns or six colors for different tendencies or four standards to describe your behaviors. But it's more effective to define your own—it helps to develop your own awareness and authenticity—before you know it, you're stranded in another predefined conformity.

2. *Add a few more:* When you think you are done, try to write down a few more. What do you see yourself doing when someone high in hierarchy approaches you? What do you see yourself doing when someone gives you feedback? What do you do when your manager challenges your presentation on which you worked really hard?

3. *Choose One:* Read your list and choose the most frustrating one.

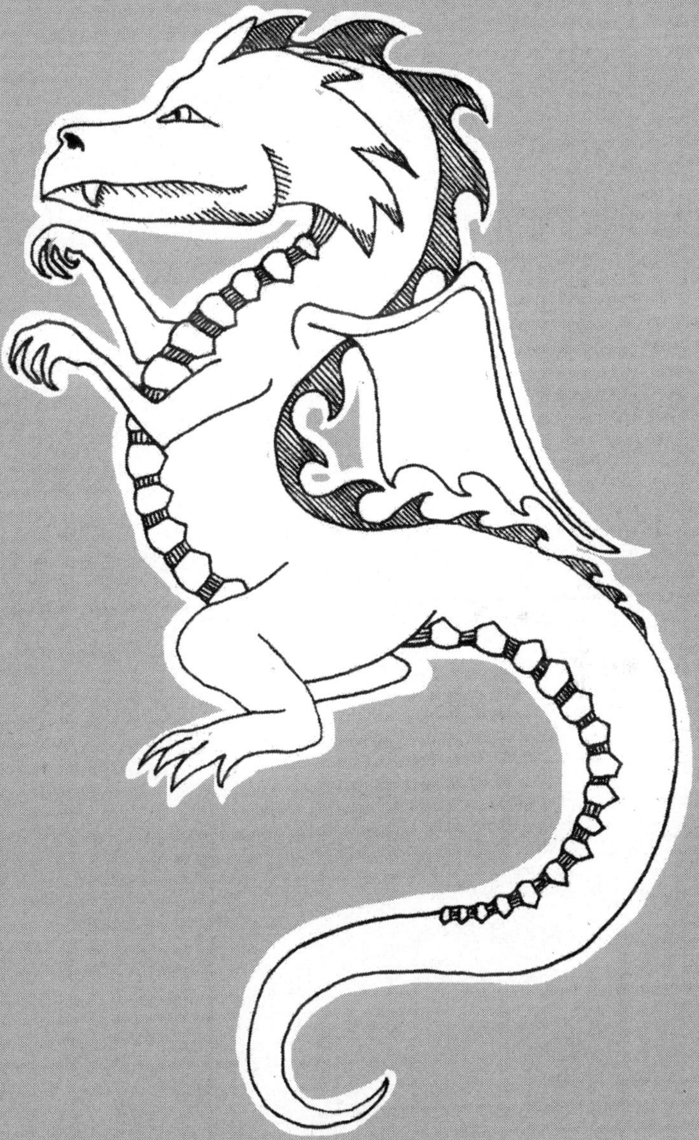

Congratulations! You just caught your dragon. It was able to do its work anonymously, but not anymore, especially if you will put the next tips into practice.

Six tips to master your dragon

These six tips will help you to raise your awareness and tame your dragons. I can honestly say that these six tips freed me from strong reactive tendencies and helped me to be myself again in challenging environments. And not only I, but my clients, use these tips to practice within their own workplaces, with amazing results.

1. *Own your dragon:* Acknowledge the fact that it is *your* reaction to the situation. It's not the situation, it's not the circumstances, and it's not the other person(s) who is to blame. Let them deal with their own dragons. You and only you can influence your reaction to this situation. So each time you encounter your dragon, acknowledge it to be yours and realize it's an opportunity for you to learn from. It's such a relief to develop from a victim into an influencer of the situation. Believe me, this change of perspective changes everything. It's the first step in regaining the lead.

2. *Name your dragon:* Don't let this dragon do its work anonymously. Give this beast a name that suits its function. Any metaphor will help since it directly visualizes the mechanism. I've heard *Calimero, Mini-me, Chameleon, Madhouse, Ice Queen, Addict, Dictator, Mrs. Rigid, Under the Carpet,* etc. Each time when your dragon is triggered and makes you react, you can at least identify it. When I do this naming exercise in training programs, I ask the participants to introduce themselves using their new dragon names. It sounds silly, but it exactly represents the dynamic between our two sides, our dragon and our authentic core—we are two differ-

ent people. Most of the time, we identify ourselves with this tendency, so in giving it another name than our own, it helps in letting go of our identification with it.

3. *Observe your dragon*: not once or twice ... at least 1000 times. You do not have to let this tendency go overnight. That only happens in fairy tales. These dragons are glued into your system. So just observe and research how your dragon takes over the steering wheel in many different situations at work and in other social situations. And remember that people who try to get rid of their dragons too fast are disappointed. The pressure to change it right away blurs our understanding of how this dragon works. Only by understanding this dragon's nature really well, can we raise our influence. What triggers your dragon? Who triggers your dragon? What does your dragon make you do or not do? What is your dragon trying to avoid?

4. *Be compassionate to your dragon*: These dragons have always protected you very well. So you can be grateful. You don't have to be mad about it or have judgments about the fact that you're acting a certain way again (and again). Approach your reactive tendency with loads of compassion. Remember, if you chop its head off, it comes back three-headed.

5. *Use your humor*: While observing it 1000 times, let your humor prevail over your harshness about yourself. Laugh when you see yourself reacting like that over and over again. When I write this, I see myself sitting in a meeting room a few years ago, attending a crowded discussion while smiling about my dragon desperately trying to defend me. I felt my strong tendency to blend in, to be careful sharing opposing opinions, since there were a lot of re-

spected colleagues present who, let's be honest, could also be quite rude sometimes. I felt my dragon arising and for the first time, I could really laugh about what it made me do. *Yes, Anke, there you go again. We've seen this happening before.* Your laughter and humor release the tension of the moment and make you more relaxed and able to observe the situation with an open mind.

6. *Choose one dragon at a time to focus on:* it works best if you focus on one dragon at a time. Yes, it's difficult for our impatient dragons who make you want to do everything perfectly and as fast as possible!

It takes time to master your dragon. After you study the way your dragon operates thoroughly, you will be able to better identify that moment between stimulus and response. Once you identify that, you can take your time and choose your response. Either you benefit from this dragon that can come in handy at times, or you choose to express your authentic core, with its own opinions, needs, and truths. The important difference is that *you* are in the lead instead of *your fears.*

You want to get more insight in your dragons? The chapter *Courage to Lead from Within* dives a little deeper and suggests helpful practices.

Lifelong learning: Switching between different states of mind

The last part of this chapter uncovers a truly important part that prevents us from getting stuck again and again. I first heard about this concept in my late twenties at the Pulsar Institute, and I am still drawing important life lessons from it. I believe this learning process will continue my entire life.

Unaware or Aware

The idea is simple: We are living our lives either aware or unaware. We are run by either creative or reactive patterns. We live our lives either trusting life and approaching it with an open mind or believing in illusions, trying to force things. This concept is derived from the knowledge of George Ivanovich Gurdjeff, a well-traveled philosopher and teacher in the twentieth century. His theory is based on the insight that most of us live our lives in "waking sleep" and we don't realize it. Think about how much time we are living in our thoughts, which are run on our automatic pilot. Think about how much time we fill with browsing in a virtual world on our smartphones. In this sleeping state of mind, our reactive patterns are in the lead, and we are automatically drawn to fit into a certain image.

In the awake state of mind, however, we lead from within. We are able to stand out in our own way and aren't troubled by unrealistic insecurities, thoughts or emotions. Several models, like the levels of leadership and system performance by Bob Anderson and Bill Adams,[37] are derived from the same way of thinking.

---

[37] Robert J. Anderson, Bill Adams, and William A. Adams, Mastering Leadership: An Integrated Framework for Breakthrough Performance and Extraordinary Business Results, (John Wiley & Sons, 2016)

Gurdjeff states that we operate from four different levels of awareness, four states of mind, and if we want to be in the lead, it's important to understand where we hang out. People who want to stand out invest time in developing their awareness.

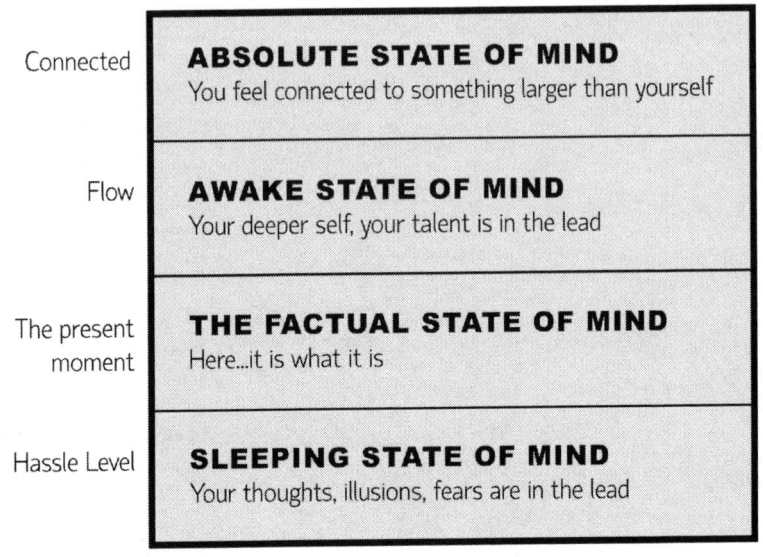

Connected	**ABSOLUTE STATE OF MIND** You feel connected to something larger than yourself
Flow	**AWAKE STATE OF MIND** Your deeper self, your talent is in the lead
The present moment	**THE FACTUAL STATE OF MIND** Here...it is what it is
Hassle Level	**SLEEPING STATE OF MIND** Your thoughts, illusions, fears are in the lead

Awareness Levels by Georges Gurdjeff

I will explain each state of mind briefly:

1. The sleeping state of mind

What is this state of mind about? This is the hassle level. It is where your limiting stories and your dragons rule your lives. It is what Brené Brown calls "the place where unconscious storytelling becomes our default." The outside world and its demands are leading you. You react from your ego, emotions, fears, status, or illusions. Your defense systems influence all your thinking and behaviors. Sometimes the reality is just too hard, too stressful, or there are too many distractions (like smartphones, social networks, or work). You surrender yourself to your old fears (the past) or to illusions of how your life should be (the future). You are escaping the reality of the current moment.

How do you notice you're operating from this state of mind? You notice that you are living in this state of mind when you have judgments, blame others, gossip, worry, have doubts, overreact, make yourself smaller or bigger, feel sorry for yourself, or chase illusions. Also, addictions or other ways of numbing your emotions fall into this category. Your flight or fight impulses and dragons are in the lead. You are just busy with surviving and your autopilot is running overtime.

2. The factual state of mind

What is this state of mind about? When someone operates from this state, they acknowledge "this is the situation I am in." They don't fly off into an imaginary world or label the facts and events that come their way with opinions, thoughts, emotions, or judgments. It's just the dry facts. This seems to be an emotionless level. It certainly isn't, because feelings do exist. You just don't let them overwhelm you. You allow them and feel them as they are—regardless of how painful or overwhelming they might be.

How do you notice you're operating from this state of mind? You see the world as it really is. You experience things as they are with an open mind. You communicate without emotions or judgments attached to it. You listen to what others tell you and hear the message without noise or without the urge to react immediately.

3. The awake state of mind

What is this state of mind about? Here, your creative mind takes the lead. Instead of the outside world ruling your behaviors, you draw inspiration from your inner world. No need to hide behind masks; you can show your true colors and be authentic. Instead of approaching the world looking through eyes full of old assumptions, you see with clear eyes. You are aware of your own unique value to the outside world. You have unique creative ideas and genuine insights and you are led by your purpose. When Karin Bakker, CEO/CCO ad interim, experienced this state of mind for the first time, she experienced a new sense of freedom, "My desire for freedom didn't involve owning fast cars and big money, but involved releasing the tension I felt inside and involved experiencing this immense freedom within myself." Her shriveled core had woken up and wanted to be in the lead again.

How do you notice you're operating from this state of mind? You feel free instead of captured by emotions or other suffocating feelings. Your judgments are erased by a sense of compassion and love. In this state of mind, creative intuitive hunches enter your mind to share with your surroundings.

4. The absolute-consciousness state of mind

What is this state of mind about? This is the highest state of mind where you feel connected to something larger than yourself. It's hard to describe, because it doesn't fit into our logic thinking. Some people call this the universe, the field, God, or nature. It is a source you can tap into, where you get your inspiration from. It refers to what the Hindu call *darshan*, the Sanskrit word for glimpse or apparition, when you see the essence of something while having a momentary connection to the divine.

How do you notice you're operating from this state of mind? You ecstatically experience the world as one in the sense that everything is connected. You feel carried or guided by a greater force that you don't have the urge to control; instead, you surrender to the natural flow of life. You have a global vision. You understand how your (and your organization's) actions affect other systems, and you try to work towards a healthy eco-system.

Please keep in mind that everyone, no matter how enlightened they are, constantly switches from one state of mind to the other. Like Paolo Coelho writes in his book *Eleven Minutes*, "Life moves very fast. It rushes us from heaven to hell in a matter of seconds." During one day, you'll switch from the sleeping state of mind to the factual, to awake and back again, but it's all about recognizing where you hang out and how that is affecting the things you do.

It's all about becoming aware and learning to influence your own state of mind. Because "Growth must be chosen over and over again. Fear must be overcome again and again." – Abraham Maslow.

An example: Mike's challenging meeting

Mike is going to a meeting where challenging decisions are supposed to be made about one of his important projects. These examples show how Mike's state of mind affects the result's meeting.

A sleeping state of mind: When he walks towards the meeting room, he already has a lot of negative thoughts in place. He is sure that John will overtake the stage by listing all his achievements in the previous projects like he always does. He is sure that his manager, Angie, who seems to be best friends with John, will not support him the way he deserves. He worked incredibly hard on this project. He starts to guard himself against possible rejection. Before he even enters the room, he is telling himself he will never reach a manager-level position since he is just not one of the bragging boys.

Mike is clearly operating from the sleeping state of mind, right? If the other participants operate from that level as well, this meeting will be ineffective. Some may try to control the situation with their dominant ideas; others may not dare to express their true opinions and ideas. People will interrupt each other. Instead of really listening, people will mostly download facts in order to react and make their own points. Eventually, the boldest one will probably win, and people like Mike will let it go or will have to influence decision-making using backdoors.

A factual state of mind: This is merely a meeting with six people working at the same company. They have the task to make a decision in order to meet a certain deadline. Each participant has different goals. Mike acknowledges his sense of fear beforehand and acknowledges the effect of his own dragon reacting in John's presence: backing off because of jealousy.

When Mike is operating from this state of mind, he acknowledges he is affected by his dragons and limiting stories. He also recognizes that stress affects the decision-making during the meeting, although he is not yet able to influence this stress the way he wants.

An awake state of mind: Mike is five minutes early to prepare. He rearranges the sloppy meeting room because he knows a clear room helps the participants to have a clear mind. The first people enter the room chatting and setting up their laptops to catch up with a few emails. Seeing their scattered minds, he suddenly gets an idea: What if he starts the meeting by showing the red- and blue pill scene from the *Matrix* movie?

When people hear him introducing it, they are surprised but, their curiosity make sure their attention is in the room instead of their devices pulling them elsewhere. He kicks off with this philosophical movie scene, where main character Neo is offered to select between a blue pill and a red pill by rebel leader Morpheus. The red pill allows him to see the harsh reality and escape from the generated dream world. The blue pill offers Neo the opportunity to remain blissfully ignorant of the illusionary world in which he lives.

After this film scene, Mike facilitates a short discussion on what the participants would do if they would were Neo and how this fragment relates to their own organization's situation. This conversation creates an open mindset which is needed to really understand the main purpose of his presentation. When decisions have to be made, he notices everyone's willingness to hear what everyone else has to say. Mike is even curious as to what John suggests drawing from his experience of previous projects.

The interesting thing is that even if only one person is operating from the awake state of mind, he or she can elevate the whole meeting and prevent failure. Hindu priest Dandapani uses an excellent metaphor to explain this principle. Imagine a napkin. Imagine you stand in the middle of the napkin and the other participants each stand in one corner. If you elevate the discussion, you move the napkin upward from the center and you elevate the others with you. One genuine remark or original action can wake up this fixed situation and reconnect the participants with their creativity instead of their reactivity.

A CEO I met a few years back always starts his important board meetings with five minutes of silence. It's his way of making sure everyone in the room can undo themselves from their own judgments and be able to reconnect with themselves instead of identifying with their dragons.

An absolute-consciousness state of mind: The week before the meeting, Mike experiences several occasions in which he is constantly witnessing conflicts, not only at work, but also at his children's school and even on the tennis court. One night he is thinking about it: there are too many conflicts to ignore. It is almost impossible to ignore the bigger picture revealed to him. The next morning, he decides to use his important decision-making meeting to make a change and discuss various ways of dealing with conflict. His openness inspires the people who are present, and together they identify two underlying issues that might cause their own ongoing conflicts within their organization. They decide on a plan how to transform these issues. The leadership Mike shows in uncovering these issues does not go unnoticed by Angie.

How to escape unawareness?

You may be wondering: *How do I jump from one state of mind to the other?* In these last few pages of Part I, I will provide you with insights to release yourself from *the asleep state of mind* into *the factual state of mind*. When you really want to stand out, you want to level up from the *factual* to the *awake state of mind*. I'll provide examples on how to do that in Part II of this book (See the chapter *Courage to Lead from Within*).

To escape *the sleeping state of mind*, we have to leave our mental state of being, our seemingly comfortable place where we make up stories to survive in the short term. We need a wake-up call to open ourselves to the current moment. Our ego and illusions need to make room for the actual reality. We want to see with clear eyes instead of eyes blurred with emotions that make us instantly react. I advise my clients to do three things:

Use the body: In this *sleeping state of mind*, we are merely living inside our mind, imprisoned by emotions, fears, or self-pity without noticing our bodily sensations. As soon as we start feeling actual sensations in our body, we leave our mental place. I know a lot of people who experience a change in their state of mind after they've been running. Their body takes over, and they notice they are free of their thoughts. I remember the change from feeling stressed to feeling relaxed after horseback riding. I was so nervous to fall off that I had to focus fully on the present moment to make sure my body and the horse did things right. I had no other choice than to leave my thoughts and worries behind me.

Although running and horseback riding definitely help, I regularly advise bodywork like yoga for clients. Well-taught yoga adds another layer where we learn to observe actual feelings, instead of having judgments about them, which is a very important part of being in the *factual state of mind*.

Use math: Use math? I agree, this seems strange, but it really is helpful. In the middle of a fight or self-pity moment, our self-defense system is very strong. A simple thing like mathematics helps to do the trick. I found out about the usefulness of math during a performance review. One of the most awful moments for people with a strong urge to fit in is being evaluated by others. After my boss complimented me on lots of things, he gave one point of critique that (of course) overshadowed all of the positive points: "You have to be more visible in the organization," he said.

Well, I hadn't had much sleep because of a stressful week, which caused me to bathe in *the sleeping state of mind*, and the tension of this conversation encouraged my tendency, crying, to take its place on the main stage. Suddenly, I got the amazing idea to do math: 849+713. This equation dragged me out of the mud of self-pity because it took all of my attention, and it shifted my mind towards factual things.

After solving the problem, I became less emotional and more rational—I could see the facts as they were. His remark wasn't an offense. It was just advice. I was even able to say "thank you." And believe me, I am not opposed to people crying and sharing their emotions, but in this case my tears weren't about his remark, they were about past critical remarks that had nothing to do with this current conversation.

Wake up the neutral observer in yourself: Like Michelangelo said, "Your own assumptions are the windows you are seeing through. Clean them once in a while. Otherwise the light will not shine in." The most sustainable way of moving up a state of mind is to practice acknowledging the situation you're in. It's not just accepting the situation you're in, it's *seeing the situation as it really is*. Not making it more beautiful, not making it more depressing. Wake up the neutral observer within you. Learn to observe your situation in a neutral way with the plusses and the minuses. Just acknowledge the facts without judgments. Face it, this is what it is right now, even when it makes you incredibly sad, angry, or frustrated.

One of my teachers, Jouke Post, has taught me how to be as neutral as possible. I had the tendency to hide the truth in my communication with a lot of smiles, diminutives, or exaggerations. I learned that I drowned in my own sadness, fear, insecurity or anger; how it all clouds the truth. After I practiced being a neutral observer, I experienced the freedom that comes with the release of those emotions.

When I taught my client Tara to wake up her neutral observer, I started by asking what kept her mind busy. Constant conflicts in her team had worried her for over a month. "The people around me are so harsh. They don't realize I have feelings too. It makes me feel extremely tired and sad."

After she actually acknowledged the fact that she, herself, let herself sink in her drama, she allowed genuine tears to flow, which was a rare thing for Tara. But after one minute, she felt relieved, and her vision wasn't blurred by creating dramatic scenes anymore. She started to dissect the situation within her team, and instead of taking it personally, she was able to understand the dynamics. By observing neutrally, she, step by step, realized how her own harshness affected her team members and made them react the same way in turn.

In Part I, you've read about fitting in. You are halfway towards standing out and showing up as yourself at work. By now you've learned about what fitting in really means. You've learned how we are wired biologically, culturally, and psychologically. Finally, I hope you and your work benefit from reading about the three different approaches to release yourself from your urge to fit in, when you don't want to.

I honestly hope you start observing yourself at work. I hope you question your limiting stories. I hope you'll identify, observe, and love your dragons until you can take back the lead for yourself and they take the backseat. I hope you see the immense power of knowing from what state of mind you operate. I hope with all my heart that you start seeing how this fitting in affects you, because it's all necessary preparation to stand out at work—and it's essential to enduring the tension of being authentic and to having the courage to create significant change.

There was no shield, no shame, no holding back.
He shared his wholeness in abundance.
He was standing out.

PART II
STANDING OUT

The thick red curtains opened majestically. The rhythm of the music instantly enchanted me as the first dancers entered the stage. The movements combined with the tunes of the music always fascinated me, and this night at the Oregon Ballet wasn't any different. How did they manage to move that elegantly while performing incredible athletic jumps?

All the dancers were skilled dancers, but my eyes were glued to one dancer in particular. He was different. He showed joy within the deep sadness. The next moment, he was tough but elegant. Was such contrast even possible? He wasn't trying to dance "prettily," he portrayed every emotion the ballet piece intended to show. That dancer, Michael Linsmeier, fascinated me. He had Talent with a capital T.

A few weeks later, I got the chance to interview him and asked, "What would be your true Talent in one word?" I am fond of this question because it helps people to learn about the essence of their Talent. He grinned and said, "I guess it is best described as... F*ck it! Give it all you got! Why not just explode and let it all out?"

Needless to say, he used more words than one, however, he described exactly what I had seen during his performance. He was not holding back at all. He showed everything—not only the lighter things, but also the darker side. There was no shield, no shame, no holding back. He shared his wholeness in abundance. He was standing out.

Michael stood out in significance. He was different, and by being different, he made a difference. People who stand out are doing their work in the sweet spot of their authenticity. They do what they are.

People who express their authentic gifts are of great value to our society. They are the influencers, creative minds, and inspirations for others. Seeing Michael dance inspired me to start writing this book. His explosion of "give it all you got!" made me want to encourage others to start tapping into their own incredible ability to stand out and make a difference, each in their own way. Every one of us can be authentic autonomous leaders in our field, feeling confident and vulnerable at the same time. Because only when we share our ultimate strengths do we feel really alive while working. No holding back. Let's start standing out together.

You, too, can stand out.

People who
stand out
are doing their
work in
the sweet spot of
their authenticity.

They do what they are.

SIX — EVERYONE CAN BE OUTSTANDING—YES, EVERYONE

I know what you're thinking. Am I really that person who could be a great powerful leader with a large audience who enjoys the spotlight over and over? You may be, you may not be. But standing out isn't about the size of your audience. It isn't about being powerful as we have come to know powerful. It isn't about being noticed.

It's about creating meaning rather than outer success. If you want to stand out, you do not have to scream. If you want to be seen, you do not have to over-perform. You do not have to cross boundaries that are not healthy for you. It isn't about being deliberately strange or dressing peculiar. You don't have to become someone you are not. You stand out by being you—100 percent You.

Everyone can stand out.

But we can't stand out in everything. We can only really shine in the field of our signature strength, because we are simply the best at that one specific thing. When we are operating from the sweet spot of our unique value, it is magnetizing. It is our trademark, and our trademark is easier to discover than just being authentic because what does "being authentic" actually mean? If you get to know the unique Talent that makes you stand out, and you learn to express it, you'll find that authenticity will come naturally along the way. In that sense, discovering your unique Talent is a good first step to living an authentic life.

The wonderful thing is that we don't have to study books for our Talent to be honed. No, everything we need is already inside of us. To stand out you do not adjust or change yourself, but change into yourself. Therefore, it's more about becoming aware of all the hurdles, masks, shields, and tricks we surround our selves with.

When I introduced the concept of Talent to poet Joseph Chicarelli, he listened and then responded, "I recognize feelings of flow—those moments where I am making something of meaning. I call them moments of clarity."

I appreciate his description. Moments of clarity are times where your Talent is switched on. You are creating with an easiness instead of trying really hard. You are acting from inside rather than reacting to something that is outside. Everything that comes from within is authentic, and others are inevitably touched by this uniqueness.

He added, "Those moments of clarity are very honest. I'll just shoot it off. Those poems are the ones I get the best feedback on. It usually trumps a specific style. It comes from a place of sincerity."

Everyone has a Talent that, if identified, expressed, and nurtured, will make them stand out. This Talent is not only given to those that we consider successful, like CEOs or famous celebrities, but to each and every one of us. So rather than think that someone isn't talented enough, recast those thoughts to, "They haven't found their unique Talent yet."

You have a unique Talent, as does your neighbor and your colleague. Regardless if you are an introvert or extravert, rational or hypersensitive, you have something special inside. Regardless if you are the boss or the employee or a volunteer. Regardless if you were blessed with an enriching childhood or you had a difficult youth. Regardless of your level of education or the amount of money in a bank account, everyone is a natural at something. Everyone has the ability to stand out in their own unique way. Everyone has a Talent. I deliberately use a capital T because your Talent is the root of all your other abilities.

Talent with a capital T

Your Talent is something you are amazingly good at. It is your signature strength. It is that something that you bring to the table like no one else can because it is your natural way of being. It's that something you add to any situation if you don't allow your thoughts or the fears or other limiting behaviors described in the first part of this book to interfere. Your Talent is the most profound "something" that defines who you are. It is an inborn ability that is available when all the defense mechanisms are lying low. Your Talent is the root of your authenticity.

You might recognize Talents within other people. Consider this: if you were to start a project and could choose your own team members, who would you invite and why?

Perhaps you would choose someone like Daniel, a real *Implementer*. He brings ideas to reality by connecting them with the right people in a way that makes it seem easy every time. Maybe you would choose to invite someone like Maya, who is a *Bearer of Multiple Perspectives*. In past discussions facilitated by her, you've found that she makes sure that several points of view are included. You also might not want to underestimate the Talent of Peter. He is a *Calmer*. He has a certain demeanor about him so that in stressful situations you know he will ease people and keep the focus on the right things.

And, in case this is a new, innovative project, you might want to include someone like my friend Godelieve. She is an *Icebreaker*. She is the first one to clear the road for others to follow easily. She breaks the ice in challenging meetings, which allows everyone to focus on what needs to be done instead of being distracted by the tension.

Of course, you would also ask them for their important content expertise, knowledge, and experience, but if you also addressed their Talent, you'd notice their eyes light up. By acknowledging your colleagues' Talents, your organization will reap the best results by actively inviting the best from them. In addition, if they are allowed and inspired to express their natural Talent on your project, you may be surprised by how engaged they will become.

Even if you don't have the luxury of choosing your team members yourself, it's still worthwhile to notice your team members' Talents and to find out how they can make a difference.

Uncovering unused potential

Lori Harris, a senior director in a Fortune 100 company, told me how one remark hit her out of the blue. Her manager shared his impression that she would be capable of much more than she showed at the moment. He believed in her, even more than she believed in herself at that time. He saw her hidden "rough edges." For Lori's manager it may have seemed a small remark, but for her, it was empowering and meant a turning point in her career.

As a leader, you can make a huge difference by taking the time to really see your employees and recognize in them their potential. It seems to be a cliché, but take a few minutes to think about it. What might be their hidden unused potential? Maybe he or she doesn't stand out yet, but what would it take to get there?

In Lori's case, it made her reflect on what her contribution could be. It unleashed a whole lot of unused, worthwhile potential for herself and for her company. When I asked her what her unique talent is, she answered instantly: "I am good with puzzles, let's put it that way. I see connections between seemingly unconnected things. And that is true for business and strategy and it's equally true in my interaction with people."

FAQ about Talent

Do I have more than one Talent?

You have many skills and strengths, which some people call talents. Your DNA provided you with these, and during the course of your life, you have developed several extra competencies. Even your defense mechanisms turn into valuable skills and strengths. All the competencies you've developed throughout your life are extremely valuable and most help you to fit in really well, but your Talent is the thing to share if you really want to make a difference. It is what only you can offer.

So the answer to whether you have more than one Talent is actually "no." There only is one way to describe your natural way of being. You are born with it, and it defines who you are at your core. Fundamentally, your Talent is the authentic root of all your skills and attitudes. It is what defines your being. It's subtle but super strong. Two people can be good piano players, but the way they stand out is different. One can bring you to tears with their playing, while the other one may be energizing. Making a difference isn't about skills—it's not about knowing the steps, it is *how you do the steps*. Both players put a piece of themselves into the performance that resonates with the audience. Our Talent is about what we can bring to the stage that is something from within.

Does this Talent really exist?

Ten years ago, I got taught to help people identify their Talent by trainers who have been helping people identifying their authenticity for over 30 years. Every time I do this, I am amazed by the effect. It's like people are finally discovering their long-lost treasure. Of course, some people ask me: "How come you're sure that everyone is born with a unique Talent?" This is a valid question. I have asked that question myself several times. However, I do not need any scientific research to know the effect it had on me and hundreds of others who I have seen blossom after discovering their Talent. Their life and the way they work took such a turn, it is hard to ignore.

Kimberley's transformation is an example that has astonished me. When I first met her, she was fed up with her organization. She was ready to quit her job and was exhausted by her attempts trying to survive in the corporate environment where she worked. Kimberley felt as if she had two choices: turn herself into someone who would fit into the standard corporate director profile, ticking off all the competencies boxes; or two, leave the company and work for a small firm or a school.

An intense period of self-reflection, self-care, and observing of her dragons followed. Immediately after she identified her Talent, tears welled up in her eyes. Kimberley identified her Talent as being a *Matriarch*. The reason she was touched by this realization was that she had been ignoring these strong feelings of care and affection for a very long time. She felt they didn't have a place in the alpha-dominated corporate environment she worked in. The system didn't exactly invite this Talent to be exposed, so for a long time she decided to work to ignore it. But while doing so, she turned into someone she didn't recognize or admire.

Kimberley was fed up with her behavior and decided to give herself a chance. That decision also meant that she would give her Talent a chance. A period of personal research began. She commenced by observing discussions. Her old self would feel inclined to immediately add her opinions, but now she just sat back and observed those in the room. She started sensing on a whole different level. She sensed the despair in the room. She saw how people were covering that despair with loud voices and strong, fixed opinions. Allowing herself the time to observe awakened her feelings of care and affection. She discovered how her Talent actually had a place in this competitive environment; how on a deeper level, it actually screamed for it. You could feel the unease wafting through the walls. Teams were communicating poorly. The only reason why this disorder hadn't yet showed itself in the business outcomes was due to the fact that everyone worked long hours.

With one foot in her comfort zone, working the way she was used to—dealing with the internal politics and adapting herself—and the other foot in the stretch zone, she developed the courage to work in a way that allowed her Talent to shine, which really started to make a difference. She never had to change her job. In fact, she became a magnet for people who brightened up working with her. Kimberley had an eye for the human side of business, knew how to create genuine connections, and wasn't scared to gather the expertise of others. She learned how to create high-performance teams by scouting for the Talents she thought were needed. From her new way of working, she was able to transform the business environment into a much healthier one.

There is also Tina's transformation. I got to know Tina as a woman who always was taking care of others, working as a caregiver to the elderly. She seemed obedient and always out to please, but she didn't feel worthy of being on the receiving end. Amidst her frustrations, she registered herself for an intense self-development program. After an in-depth period of self-reflection and self-care, she uncovered emotions and progressed from despair to hope. Finally, she was able to transform into a proud woman.

Tina identified her Talent as *Tension Releaser*, which gave her the right amount of confidence to begin experimenting with her Talent. By asking the right questions in brief conversations, she was able to release their tension, often while using humor. In fact, she found that humor enhanced the effectiveness of her Talent. As Tina's confidence grew, she began to wear different clothes and act a different way. Tina even discovered that she loved to perform stand-up comedy. Who would have thought that before she went through this transformation?

I noticed her Talent during one of her spontaneous comedy performances. We all laughed to tears as she dissected organizational dynamics nobody dared to speak of. Now, she still works as an excellent caregiver and uses her Talent to light up the days of many elderly.

What a waste it would have been if Kimberley's and Tina's (and everyone else's) Talents remained undiscovered. Think of a pumpkin seed. The whole blossoming plant that is about to share its fruit is already within that one seed. When the circumstances are right, the wonders of what is stored inside come out. In our case, it's just like that—when the circumstances are right and we allow ourselves to discover what's inside, our blueprint is capable of something unique. Wouldn't it be incredible if each of us could unleash our full potential?

Does everyone have a different Talent?

Yes, each eye catches something different. I find this fascinating. If you observe those around you, you might notice the *Includer*, the person who always seems to include every opinion in every situation. Or the *Storyteller*, the one who tells stories and keeps everyone hanging on to each word. It would be easy to feel jealous, but the wonderful thing is that each of us has our own unique value to add to the mix. If we really realize this, we can stop competing and comparing ourselves to others and start working together, just as in nature everything has its own value and works together. Think of the different qualities of the Sun and the Moon; every one of us has incredible value to add in our own way and at our own time.

If we really would understand this fact, our conversations with peers could transform into refreshing ones. I like sharing experiences with other coaches, but I used to end up in a subtle contest to see who would do the most amazing work. When I was finally fed up with this underlying competitive struggle, I started to ask different questions, such as: "In what specific thing do you really stand out?" Or "When did you really make a difference and how?" The whole conversation immediately transformed from trying to prove one's own value to exploring each other's value.

How great it would be to know who to turn to in what situation? The person who brings *Order in Chaos* just naturally knows what to do to erase the confusion. The *Safe Haven* creates trust within the team, and you feel recharged after their Talent interventions. The *Vision Keeper* provides others with inspiring future opportunities. We all stand out in our own unique way. Rumi wrote:

> Each of us has been made for some particular work, and the desire for that work has been put in every heart.

Now, imagine three of your team members for a moment. What would be their Talent? What is their signature strength? Imagine what would happen if they would be able to express the particular work that's been put in their heart. If we all took the time to look further than the standard scripts and work descriptions, I am sure we would find the added value that everyone brings to our clients, projects, and profits.

A few years ago I, was asked by our CEO to use my Talent to solve a conflict. He always intuitively knew to put the right Talent in the right place. Now, one of our clients at the Leadership Institute had backed out. Misunderstandings had led to conflicts that were hard to overcome, so the client decided to terminate the contract. It was a huge contract involving dozens of training programs each year. Our clients were quite angry and disappointed, not really willing to open the conversation once more.

Our CEO sensed that my natural response would lighten up the tense situation, and he was right. Taking my Talent as a starting point, I knew what to say at the right moment. I could create a genuine connection while melting their initial resentment. It was such a pleasure to help save this deal, mostly because we could mend our connection with this client and not leave things unresolved. Besides it being a smart decision from him to look for the right Talent within the organization, my boss provided me a moment to shine and to feel helpful.

How is our Talent activated?

Each Talent is a solution for something else. We have an antenna to detect those situations that ask for our Talent.

Rumi wrote about this phenomenon:

I've said before that every craftsman
searches for what's not there
to practice his craft.

A builder looks for the rotten hole
where the roof caved in.
A water carrier picks the empty pot.
A carpenter stops at the house with no door.

Workers rush toward some hint
of emptiness, which they then
start to fill.

When our Talent is confronted with an emptiness, it automatically begins to fill that hole. My teacher Jan de Dreu's Talent is *Teacher*. How bizarre, right? He has an irresistible urge to look for people in situations who are not yet learning. He is almost irritated by people who overlook their learning opportunities, but it switches his heart "on" and his Talent starts to do its thing.

Like him, our Talent is activated by its opposite. When our antenna receives signals of an emptiness, our Talent is endlessly creative and is able to come up with interventions to fill that void. *In what situations is your switch turned on? What emptiness do you naturally want to fill?*

Rumi also wrote:

There is one thing in this world which you must never forget to do.
If you forget everything else and not this, there is nothing to worry about.

But if you remember everything else and forget this, then you will have done nothing in your life.

Your Talent is your way of providing value to the world. It is how you make a difference in the best possible way. According to Immanuel Kant, it is our duty to cultivate our Talent to contribute to society. We should make the effort to expand and improve our fortunate natural predispositions.

Will I have to change my career?

The majority of people have chosen their jobs based on their dragons instead of their Talent. But what should you do if your newly identified Talent doesn't seem to fit your job? Let's look at Caroline's case. She worked her way up by relying on her "tough cookie" negotiating skills, until she identified her Talent as *Shelter from the Storm*. She wondered, "How on earth could me being a *Shelter from the Storm* be of value in future negotiations?" After all, she mostly relied on her shrewdness in making sharp deals.

Caroline decided to stay on and see how things would progress. Step by step, she discovered how she could either choose her Talent or her dragon to enter the stage and influence the situation accordingly. Instead of her dragons taking over unconsciously as they had done previously, now she Kindly held their reins and assessed the situation first. In Caroline's situation, this increased versatility led to an expansion of her job. Her manager saw how she had matured within the last months and gave her more team responsibilities.

Caroline's example shows why I always encourage people to stay, at least for a while, and see how they can transform their current job in such a way that their Talent really can start making a difference. In some cases, however, people need a change and they use their newly identified Talent as a compass to pinpoint their new careers.

Revitalizing any situation with our Talent

Starting off with our Talent in mind

He could hear the clock ticking in the gray meeting room. Another minute and this room was supposed to be full of smart people deciding on a strategy that would change the course of their business.

Despite a feeling of reluctance, he took his laptop, connected it to the screen, and watched as the first people came in. Some were busy with their phones, others were heartily discussing matters from a previous meeting. People were opening laptops and disappearing into their deluge of emails. This distracting buzz told him all he would get this morning was scattered attention. But in order to make good decisions, they needed focused minds.

In that moment, he hesitantly decided to follow a hunch. He cleared his voice and asked, "Please pack your belongings, stand up, and I kindly ask you to leave the room. You are invited back to the room as soon as you have cleared your minds and are able to focus on this meeting."

For a few seconds, people stared at him. Then they packed their stuff and left the room, only to reenter after a few moments.

"That was one of my most memorable moments in my career," Mason told me. It was in that moment that he became aware of his ability to impact meetings. He continued, "After everyone reentered the room, we could start with fresh minds. This pause somehow connected us and made us decide on important matters much better and quicker than before without distractions. Such a relief."

That moment, Mason gave way to his Talent, the *Vivifier*. His Talent inspired him to change the normal course of the meeting that typically would have consisted of many distractions and numerous attempts to make it work. But due to this surprising intervention, he was able to connect with his coworkers on another level, which created a positive impact on the decision-making after the intervention. He chose not to roll with the way things were usually done around there. Instead, he used his Talent to reset the atmosphere and mindset of those attending the meeting.

Be in the lead of the event, instead of the event leading you

For a long time, we believed it was better to fit into to a certain mold to belong and to meet others' expectations. Our main focus was the outside world, and with our eyes constantly fixed on how others would perceive us, we remained walking in circles trying to fit in. In most cases, we didn't believe it was better, but we did it without being fully aware that we changed ourselves to follow existing ways.

People who stand out have learned to begin with their Talent as the place to get the ball rolling instead of trying to fit into their default mold. Standing out is about finding a new "form" inspired by our authentic Talent instead of automatically fitting in that existing form. Mason realized the status quo, such as sitting in a meeting room with laptops open and divided attention, didn't work. So, he revitalized the existing form by letting the people reenter the room free from distraction and with a new mindset. Of course, this change of routine surprised people, but he gained so much more attention for his presentation, which enabled the group to make better decisions faster.

We can revitalize any situation by starting with our Talent in mind. Again and again, we are able to design new forms while doing that. A whole new area of opportunities can be explored. If you allow yourself to stand out, you will be able to lead the event instead of the event leading you.

Attending any business leadership seminar, you hear about changing the way we do business and how we need to shift current systems. If we really want to change the current systems, we need people who come up with new thinking, new forms, new ideas. We need people to start breaking the standard codes. We need people who start out with their Talent to revitalize "the way we do business." This is your chance to begin thinking of ways you can engage the next disengaging meeting. *How you can revitalize your team, your next client meeting, your next family vacation? How different would all of these experiences look if you started with your Talent in mind?*

Shifting our perspective on four domains

All our lives we are taught that we have to become someone. Isn't that strange? Aren't we already someone? Someone really special? The journey towards standing out isn't about becoming anything. It is more about unbecoming everything that isn't really you. Only then you can be who you were meant to be in the first place. To start with your Talent in mind, you have to unlearn everything that has been covering your Talent, like fears, dogmas, and unrealistic expectations in order to make room for your natural response.

It's time to unlearn many of the things we've been taught by our parents, our educators, and our culture.

After working with lots of different clients on this topic, I have observed that those who begin standing out have radically shifted their focus on four domains:

1. *Shift focus from weaknesses to strengths:* People who stand out have unlearned to focus on merely improving their weaknesses. Instead, they primarily focus on their strengths and have developed an awareness about what they are naturally good at.

2. *Shift focus from outside-in to inside-out:* People who stand out have learned to trust their inner knowledge and wisdom, rather than only gathering more knowledge from the outside.

3. *Shift focus from reacting to creating:* People who stand out have unlearned their tendencies to impulsively react to a situation. They create new scenarios instead of reacting to an existing situation.

4. *Shift focus from scoring to purpose-driven:* People who stand out have unlearned to focus on just their individual successes and their desires to score and compete with others. They reach out, contribute, and create significance to the world around them.

Let me illustrate these four shifts of perspective by sharing my own anecdote of learning to express my Talent while unlearning these habits.

When I started my new career as a trainer in the personal development programs, it felt great. Finally, I created the right circumstances to express my potential. I was exactly in the place where I wanted to be. That is, until I realized that I wasn't there yet. I had to follow up and enter the scary path of unleashing this intangible Talent that didn't come with a simple how-to guide.

During one of my first training programs, I worked with a very experienced trainer, Patrick. I admired him. He immediately connected with the participants, telling engaging stories. He assessed people on the spot. He revealed weaknesses within the first few minutes. In a way, he had a directive style. I also wanted to tell stories, with everyone eager to hear what I had to say. I also wanted to "see through" people like he seemed to be doing. As I was impatiently searching to make an impact on the participants, I found myself trying to model him and to fit into the box of the "ideal" trainer.

I wanted it all, but all I noticed was that I froze while trying to copy him. I told Patrick about my insecurities and he replied, "You know what I noticed? I can do this the way I do because you are standing next to me. I feel that you somehow carry this group. There is an enormous amount of trust built by you."

I was puzzled. I didn't understand what he meant. I remember thinking, "You shine while I'm in the background building intangible trust that no one immediately notices." Half a year later, it became clear to me. My admiration for his Talent took over my ability to trust my own Talent. Striving towards his success with participants took over sharing my own unique value. Instead of really working together, I was competing with him and working hard to stand in the same spotlight.

I became skilled in training tricks I had copied because copying was one of my best dragons. But his directive style was his cup of tea and not mine. And I didn't want to be just good enough; I wanted to be an excellent trainer and add real value.

That moment, the Talent I had identified years earlier during a week of training dawned on me. I remembered my own unique value that made me stand out—my Talent. I stand out as a *Disarmer*. Instead of being directive, I am someone whose tenderness allows those who are too are hard on themselves to soften and discover hidden truths. Although I had already identified my Talent, it took me some more time to really take it in and shake off my automatic responses and limiting thoughts.

It took time to understand that:
A. The fact that I, myself, am the best at something and that I didn't have to rely on copying others.
B. My Talent had a lot to do with tenderness—a Talent totally different from the tougher and cooler Talents like Patrick's, which are so much easier to express and tend to be more valued in a corporate setting.

But a copy is never as good as the original. I think of ourselves as paintings. The original painting is so much more valuable than the copy. People can easily distinguish the original from the fake. We have an X-ray for authenticity. I had to acknowledge this fact despite it scaring the hell out of me. I am not who I thought I wanted to be, a directive trainer, but I am very good at something else, disarming and making people feel confident in themselves.

Shift focus from weaknesses to strengths

What do you think would have happened if I had kept my focus on what was not there yet? If I had primarily focused on developing my weaknesses, for example, being more directive, I probably would have gained insight on how to be more direct, but I probably would also have ended up being an average trainer. I would have been exhausted trying to keep up and compare with the other trainers whose Talents I also would have desired to copy over and over again.

Don't get me wrong; I am a huge fan of the growth mindset versus fixed mindset introduced by Stanford psychologist Carol Dweck,[38] who states that intelligence and personality can be developed, rather than being immutably engrained traits. It's true that everyone *can* develop their weaknesses into strengths. In my case, I learned how to be more directive, which was helpful in some cases. It's good to be versatile and grow into unexplored areas, as long as those inauthentic skills don't overrule our authenticity and drive us to be someone we are not.

For a long time, our culture has had the tendency to primarily focus on us fixing what we lack, instead of focusing on and giving us room to develop our strengths. Fortunately, education systems and organization development theories are realizing we should at least focus on both. Gallup analysis reveals that people who focus on their strengths every day are three times more likely to report having an excellent quality of life, six times more likely to be engaged at work, eight percent more productive, and 15 percent less likely to quit their jobs.[39]

What would happen if you focused on what is already available within yourself and what is already available in others, even though it might not yet be expressed in its full potential? What if you would learn to value what is available in abundance and learn how to express that without holding back?

Shift focus from outside-in to inside-out

It takes a mind shift to trust that everything that makes our Talent specific is already inside of us. It is so different from the traditional

---

[38] Carol Dweck, *Mindset: The New Psychology of Success* (Random House, 2006)

[39] Brooke Fernandez and Sarah Houle, "An Effective Strengths Program: Cardinal Health Case Study" *Gallup Business Journal* (2015)

way we educate ourselves. We are used to taking in knowledge from outside sources. We are wired to learn our way in life by watching and mimicking others. "Children will copy everything that they see an adult demonstrate to them, even if there are reasons why those actions would be irrelevant," says psychologist Mark Nielsen.[40]

Our copying behavior appears to be a human factor, as they did not find the same results for similar tests with chimpanzees. So, if we are wired like this and we are taught from outside sources for over fifteen years while in school and college, it feels like this form of learning is the norm. It's no wonder that we continue to pursue this form of education until we have received every certificate we think we need.

Nonetheless, all the knowledge that's available about our specific Talent is already written inside of ourselves. Regardless, we are not used to trusting our own inner body of knowledge. Inner knowledge isn't from a book. It isn't double-checked by scientific research. Why should we trust it? Certainly, when we are operating outside our comfort zone, we look for every outside control that can keep us from failing. When we see others succeeding, we want to model that success, like I tried to do with Patrick during my first training programs. The thing is, when we trust what is already inside, that is when we can truly begin to stand out.

(Middle) Eastern traditions, like yoga and Buddhism, have affirmed the existence of inner knowledge and intuition for centuries, but somehow, in our Western society, the attachment to outer knowledge continues to prevail, which tends to overshadow our inner knowledge. In the thirteenth century, Rumi wrote about this topic.

---

[40] M. Nielsen and K. Tomaselli. "Overimitation in Kalahari Bushman Children and the Origins of Human Cultural Cognition," *Psychological Science*, May (2010)

EVERYONE CAN BE OUTSTANDING—YES, EVERYONE

Two Kinds of Intelligence

There are two kinds of intelligence: one acquired, as a child in school memorizes facts and concepts from books and from what the teacher says, collecting information from the traditional sciences as well as from the new sciences.

With such intelligence, you rise in the world. You get ranked ahead of or behind others in regard to your competence in retaining information. You stroll with this intelligence in and out of fields of knowledge, getting always more marks on your preserving tablets.

There is another kind of tablet, one already completed and preserved inside you. A spring overflowing its spring box. A freshness in the center of the chest. This other intelligence does not turn yellow or stagnate. It's fluid, and it doesn't move from outside to inside through conduits of plumbing-learning.
This second knowing is a fountainhead from within you, moving out.

When I started trusting the second kind of intelligence—the inner knowledge—I started to act authentically. I began to feel the "freshness in the center of my chest." Everything specific thing I needed to know about my Talent was written on my "own tablet preserved inside me." As soon as I learned to shift within and connected with that inner knowledge, hunches arose in my mind and I knew how to express my Talent. Nobody else or nothing else outside of me could have taught me anything about my specific authenticity.

My Talent involved listening instead of telling engaging stories like Patrick. My Talent involved giving space to underlying feelings instead of providing directive guidance. It required patience instead of speed. Believe me, some participants begged me the first training day to analyze them in search of a trainer who could steer them towards "a recipe to fix them." But when I wasn't being seduced to do so and aligned myself with my "own tablet," most of them discovered that being in a trusted environment enabled them to let their guard down and identify valuable truths about themselves.

It took guts to step out of the proven trainer tricks that I had developed (my copying-defending-mechanisms) and allow this intangible Talent inside of me to blossom. But somehow I knew this intangible Talent was right for me. It felt as if I was an autonomous human being instead of a toy swinging from left to right trying to follow the success of others. It felt authentic to rely on myself instead of others, which elevated my feeling of well-being to the next level.

Should we eliminate all outside education and burn our certificates? Should we stop learning job-specific skills? Of course not, it's good to be versatile. For each job, there are important things and skills to know and learn. We don't have to reinvent the wheel. If doctors solely relied on their Talents and didn't attend med school, we certainly would not trust them with our health. But there is a difference between doctors who merely follow protocols by the book and execute what they've learned, and doctors who connect with their patients first and give their Talent a place in the exam room. It makes a huge difference if their authentic selves are in there as well. It is what differs a human being from a robot. So go ahead, add your Talent into the mix of certificates, experience, and outside knowledge and magic will appear.

Shift focus from reacting to creating

Have you ever realized it makes a world of difference whether you react or create? The actual difference between fitting in and standing out is this difference of reaction versus creation. Either you are led by your dragons, who make you react impulsively, or you are inspired by your Talent, which is incredibly creative? Reacting to the situation can have multiple forms. Remaining a silent observer, thinking about what you could've done in a situation, might mean that you are not impulsively responding, but neither are you joining in. You are not creating a new scenario, or transforming the situation.

In my case, I tried to change myself at first in order to fit in. That was my reaction to the situation. I took the situation for granted and made sure I adapted to the standards already present. But by bringing my Talent into play, I added my unique value to transform the situation and create a whole new scenario. We are like a school of fish: we either swim with the tide or we decide to change the course. What about you? Are you swimming with the tide or are you changing the course?

Each moment offers you a new opportunity to either react or create. You may remember the quote ascribed to Victor Frankl, the neurologist and psychiatrist I introduced earlier, "Between stimulus and response there is a space. In that space is our power to choose our response. In our response lies our growth and our freedom." Each time there is a stimulus that triggers our reaction, we can choose our response. We can mature and learn to change our focus from reactionary to creative and enable ourselves to add real value to different situations and experiences. In the last three chapters of this book, you will learn more about learning how to shift from reactionary to creative.

Look at the differences found in Luisa's story. Luisa is a customer service director. One morning she was cc-ed on an escalation email one of her peers had sent to her manager. She was irritated why certain results had not yet come through. She had two options, react to the situation or create a new scenario and add value. Let's take a look:

Option one—Luisa impulsively reacts: While reading the email, she gets annoyed and thinks, this is the third time she has written an email like this. Why won't she just come to see me instead? Luisa immediately writes back stating that if she would like an update, she needs to come and see her instead of writing stressed emails. Luisa doesn't receive an answer and continues to run around the office unaware of all the irritation she brings to each meeting, making things much harder for everyone including herself. You might imagine the ripple effect that her bad mood and her irritation causes her team throughout that day.

Option two—Luisa reflects and creates a new scenario: While reading the email, Luisa notices that she feels annoyed. To be honest, her stomach is in knots because this is the third time she has received a similar email from her colleague. She closes her eyes and takes a moment to breathe in and out. She wonders: what can I do? She decides to let this email rest until after lunch. During lunch, she gets an idea. What if I invite her to the next project meeting? Then we'll understand her context and she'll be able to understand the challenges we are facing. Later that afternoon, her colleague approaches her desk saying she is interested to join the meeting to get more insight. She is even more than willing to help out than Luisa initially figured. In that brief moment, they already co-created a short-term work-around.

When we are led by our dragons, we react impulsively to the situation. Usually, this doesn't make things better in the long run. It can be easy to get stuck within our existing reality as it is, and most times that means a vicious circle spiraling downward. If we are able to receive the reality of the situation with an open and honest mind, just as Luisa did in the second case, we also open ourselves up for inspiring solutions that originate from our Talent. We jump into the space between stimulus and response, and we can transform the reality and create new scenarios.

Shift focus from scoring to purpose-driven

When I was looking to create the best project team for a challenging rebranding project, I immediately knew who I had to include on my team. My colleague Fanny was gifted at the finishing touch and seeing important details, something in which I usually need help. Through her attention to detail, she created an enormous amount of significance for us and for the rebranding. She didn't do this for her individual benefit; rather, she added her value because she wanted to make a difference in what we presented to our client.

The Talents of countless people have helped me. In periods of sadness, I know who to turn to. When I want to be energized, I know who to call. It also works the other way around. I know my Talent has been of value for other people as well. People who are stuck, who lost touch with themselves knock on my door. How wonderful is this alliance of Talents between people? We can add value and meaning to one another in our own unique ways.

Joseph Chicarelli, the writer and a poet I interviewed, spoke rather shyly about the purpose of his writing: "People get the feeling that they are not alone. It means a lot to me. If I never get popular, those things are still going to matter."

His stories create a sense of solidarity with his readers, and it makes an impact on how they perceive themselves. These are pockets of meaning that others can receive. All of our Talent's actions are pockets of meaning. Small or big. The impact we have on people doesn't always need to be huge or vivacious.

One of my teachers, Jan de Dreu, kept telling us, "As long as your Talent touched one person's soul, you succeeded."

When you read this book's title, your first thoughts might have been that this book was about how to stand out, score, be successful, and live like a celebrity. By now, you must have realized this book is about something else. It is about standing out in significance, revitalizing your surroundings purposefully. Getting to know and understand your Talent will help you identify what makes you distinctive and may lead towards success and the freedom to be who you really are. You will have no more need to fit into a jacket that isn't yours. You have found your own jacket to wear. But most importantly, that jacket is about creating significance for your surroundings. Your Talent is the solution *you* bring to the table, rather than anyone else. It is what you have to offer to the world that matters for the world around you. It's your purpose.

In her book, *Power of Meaning*, Emily Esfahani Smith[41] explains how our society desperately looks for happiness and how this quest leads to short-term gains, but searching for meaning over the long term actually boosts psychological health.[42] Based on varying research, she encourages readers to redirect our quest for happiness towards creating significance. When we experience how our Talent actually makes a difference in someone else's life, our purpose can

---

[41] Emily Esfahani Smith, *Power of Meaning* (Crown, 2017)

[42] Veronika Huta and Richard Ryan, "Pursuing Pleasure or Virtue: The Differential and Overlapping Well-Being Benefits of Hedonic and Eudaimonic Motives," *Journal of Happiness Studies*, Volume 11, Number 6 (2009)

shift from wanting self-gain and instant happiness to wanting to make a difference. In the end, it is so much more rewarding to see a person's conflict or a situation resolved than feeling fulfilled by providing smart remarks.

Victor Frankl survived living in a concentration camp for three years. He observed how prisoners who found or maintained a sense of meaning, even in the most horrendous circumstances, were far more resilient to suffering than those who did not. The fact that life was still expecting something from them made all the difference. A man who becomes conscious of the responsibility he bears towards a human being who affectionately waits for him, or to an unfinished work, will never be able to throw away his life. He knows the "why" for his existence and will be able to bear almost any "how."[43]

---

[43] Victor Frankl, *Man's Search for Meaning*, (Verlag für Jugend und Volk, Austria, 1946)

What is your Talent with a Capital T?

SEVEN — IDENTIFYING OUR AUTHENTIC TALENT

I bet you are becoming more and more curious about what your Talent might be and how you can use it, aren't you? You might have some ideas of what your Talent could be, but even though it has been with you your whole life, your Talent has a way of hiding itself from you. Have you seen the movie *As It Is In Heaven*?[44] Gabriella, one of the main characters, sings a wonderful song about her long-lost authentic voice, "I haven't forgotten who I was. I just let it sleep." In a way, our Talent is hibernating and we can wake it up.

Children approach life in a natural way. Events that need their Talent automatically catch their eye, and they'll give their natural response. The fortunate people among us might remember a sense of feeling immensely free as children. The flow we can experience expressing our Talent without holding back resembles the same sense of freedom.

But circumstances make us leave our natural sense of being, such as rejections or remarks by our parents, teachers, classmates. As children, we are vulnerable and don't have the tools at hand to defend ourselves properly or ignore rejections like we are able to when we mature. And because our natural way is the most vulnerable piece of ourselves, our dragons are born and hide that valuable piece from us. Remember reading about all of that in Part I: Fitting In?

---

[44] *As it is in Heaven*, a Swedish film directed by Kay Pollak (2004)

Luis' early spontaneous attempts to mediate between his parents were ignored, and sometimes, he was brutally yelled at. Of course, he stopped his natural approach of building bridges from appearing. Luis started to shut down when he saw people disconnecting. Luckily, he looked for help when he was in his forties and his tendency to shut down took over his happiness. With help, he was happily surprised when he rediscovered his long-lost natural way of approaching events. Being in between people felt natural to him, but it also took some guts to augment the impact of his Talent.

After experimenting and dedicated practice, he really started to acknowledge that he actually stood out and was able to help others to reconnect. He enjoyed the smile and relief on people's faces after his interventions that helped people reconnect in meetings, at home, and many other places. He felt it made a difference, and that made him realize he made a difference.

Uncovering Talent

When Talent is hidden, it is worthwhile to uncover it. Uncovering hidden Talent requires special attention. First of all, our Talent is unique and only to be defined by ourselves. Tests, examinations, or experts can provide hints, but ultimately, I believe we are the only ones who can define the essence of it. Why? Experts and tests might be very good at identifying and sensing most strengths, but they merely perceive the sides that a person is already expressing most of the time. Also, our dragons are guarding our vulnerable treasure extremely well. We have to make sure our dragons lose their influence for a while so that our defending mechanisms will not appear in the test results representing our core strengths.

This book offers you a set of questions that will help you on the way to uncover your Talent. Although it hides itself, your Talent always has been with you. You must have experienced several moments in which you made an actual authentic difference. Just find some time to answer the questions below and you may be surprised with what rises in your mind. Of course, you can find friends, family, or colleagues to help you. They sometimes can pinpoint how you make a difference you, yourself, cannot see. However, I advise you to hear their input, but at the same time, be cautious. Their feedback is their perspective, which is sometimes blurred by relationship dynamics, and we are looking for *your* perspective.

First,

Remember these important characteristics of a Talent:

- *It's your nature:* Your Talent is the most profound quality that defines who you are. Try to erase the importance of all your competencies, skills, personality traits, and strengths from your memory during this exercise. Try to start with a blank slate. Don't worry about not including your other skills. Your most important skills will probably be supporting you to express this Talent anyway, but they are subordinate to your Talent. One of my skills is listening, and of course, I apply lots of listening while I express my Talent. I even apply my dragon skills of blending in and making the other person feel at ease, but you are looking for the top of the mountain, the first domino stone, that influences all the other stones (skills) to fall in place.
- *It's for others:* Your Talent makes you significant for others, so your Talent is only relevant in relationship to other people or events. Besides the fact that it provides meaning to your life, it's not exclusively for your own benefit. Each Talent adds value to the surrounding world in a different way.

- *It's activated on the opposite:* Your Talent is activated when you encounter the contrary. Remember how Luis' eye catches the disconnections in relationships—it's where his *Bridge Builder* is activated. When my eye catches harsh judgments, my disarming Talent is activated.
- *It's singular:* For over the last 30 years, the Pulsar Institute has worked towards recognizing each and every one's specific Talent. They've discovered that if you describe your Talent in one word, it functions as a compass. Although our Talent is extremely unique and therefore extremely complex to describe in words, the risk of not labeling your Talent is larger. When I notice my influence or added value is drifting away during a challenging meeting, all I have to do is to remind my Talent in one word and it helps me to refocus. Your unique value is way more profound than this word, but if you don't capture it, it is easily forgotten. In the past years, I've heard beautiful descriptions of people's Talents: *Vision Keeper, Teacher, Midwife, Icebreaker, Includer, Upgrader, Wonderer, Bringer of Wisdom, Safe Haven, Creating Order in Chaos, Disruptor, Trust Provider, Clarifier, Listener, Strengthener, Encourager, Optimizer, Simplifier, Adventure Guide, The Nail on the Head.* It doesn't need to be grammatically correct, as long as you attach the right meaning to it yourself.
- *It's constant:* Your Talent defines your nature, and your natural essence doesn't change in the course of your life, so what you are about to uncover remains the same. You might change some words to better describe its working, but the essence will remain the same.

Next,

Find a tangible example of an accomplishment in which *you* made a real difference. It can be something you did or initiated. It doesn't have to be anything huge, as long as you felt that you made a difference in a certain situation or in someone else's life. That tangible example can be a picture, a video, a document, or an object that symbolizes your accomplishment. For example, Kella brought a recording of a song she created for her school that led to an intense connection within the community. Ben brought a shell to represent an impactful conversation on the beach that relieved his colleague from worry. Sita brought a video of her PhD dissertation to represent her special way of working together with her research students.

When did something you did, said, or created have a significant impact on another person or situation? What tangible picture, video, document or object reminds you of this moment? Place this tangible example in front of you when answering the next questions.

Talent identification[45]

Questions connected to the tangible object:
- What was the difference you made? In other words, what would not have been created if you weren't present? You might have to think beyond any tangible results; there may have been more underlying effects caused by your accomplishment. Be honest and be proud.

---

[45] If you want to explore the essence of your Talent more deeply, go to www.anketusveld.com/mytalent and receive a 7-day complimentary Talent exercise using the codeword: makeadifference.

- What caught your eye? What triggered you to make this difference?
- What effect did it cause to the situation and/or people?

General questions:
- What kind of situations naturally catch your eye?
- What do you offer in a complex situation?
- What is the effect on the other people or situation?
- What isn't there, when you aren't in the room?

One final question:
- What comes to mind if you finish this sentence? I am a born ...
- Write down the first words that come to mind and craft a word or short sentence for your Talent that satisfies *you*. I emphasize *you*, since your dragons are likely to interfere at this point.

Congratulations, you just made your first steps in identifying your Talent! Take a few moments to realize that you make a real difference to people and situations on this area. You are able to transform complex or tough situations into better ones just by being you and by enabling your Talent to express itself. Isn't that amazing?

I advise you to cherish your newly identified Talent. You might feel like you finally discovered a long-lost treasure, but for others, their Talent isn't something that immediately sticks. My friend Sara mentioned how her newly discovered Talent felt like a young butterfly that had just emerged from its cocoon, the wings still thin and light. With this statement, she quintessentially captured the delicateness of a newly discovered Talent. You are willing to trust its value; however, it isn't established or as strong as other well-known strengths yet. Take care of the maturation of your Talent with lots of determination. Sit with your Talent for now. Don't try to change it or improve it. Give it all the trust, encouragement, and nourishment until the day your Talent is strong enough to give you wings.

You can also turn to a trained professional to facilitate you in identifying your Talent yourself. Sometimes, it's challenging to do this all by yourself as we are often hindered by images of ourselves from life experiences, results from past personality tests, or our self-judgments. Our Talent is so obvious to ourselves, we tend to overlook this specialty and reduce it to "something normal everyone does" and dismiss its value.

Besides this fact, I mentioned earlier that your Talent sometimes is hidden very well. In order to find it, it requires you to lower your guard and take the challenging, tender route inwards. During the uncovering process, our (I and many other experts who are trained to do this) sole purpose is to create the right circumstances. We enable you to connect with yourself through visualization methods in combination with other exercises. While naming your Talent, we are keen on capturing any dragon actions so they cannot interfere, and we make sure you can find the right words for your Talent. We enable you to name your Talent in your own words; we never mention the word for you.

What if you could find *ease with the uneasiness* of standing out, even in challenging moments?

EIGHT – USING OUR TALENT, ESPECIALLY WHEN IT REALLY MATTERS

As soon as people have identified their Talent and sat with it for a while to nourish it with trust, I encourage them to express that special Talent in daily life at least once a day, in any situation.

This is the moment to shift towards being led by our Talent instead of being led by our dragons and to create significant value for our surroundings. You might know the popular and relevant quote by Stephen R. Covey,[46] "Act or will you be acted upon." As soon as we remember who we essentially are, the game can change. Now we can create our game instead of playing constantly by the rules of someone else's game. It is time to show our real leadership and start to make a difference for ourselves, but more importantly, for others.

Each expression of Talent consists of four steps. These steps can actually take place naturally within a few seconds. Sometimes, you just need a magnifying glass to examine and learn something of value. A Talent intervention begins with something that catches your eye, for example, a colleague who seems to be disappointed. You hear him sigh and he drops his shoulders. Then, instead of ignoring his disappointment and going on with your own work, or reacting in a way you'll regret afterwards, you shift within and wait for a creative

---

[46] Stephen R. Covey, *The 7 Habits of Highly Effective People* (Free Press, 1989)

hunch to arise in your mind. You might suddenly feel that sitting next to your colleague could be of help. You don't necessarily know the direct benefits of this idea, but somehow your Talent inspires you with this intervention. The last step is to actually act on your hunch, in this specific example, to connect with this person by, for example, sitting next to this person and drop your own work for a minute.

First, I will introduce the basics of each step in the Talent Expression:
1. *Connecting part 1, connect to receive:* See an opportunity for your Talent to bring significance.
2. *Lead from within:* Shift your focus within and resist outside distractions.
3. *Capturing the creative hunch:* Allow a creative idea to kick in.
4. *Connecting part 2, connect to act:* Bring your hunch into reality to make a difference.

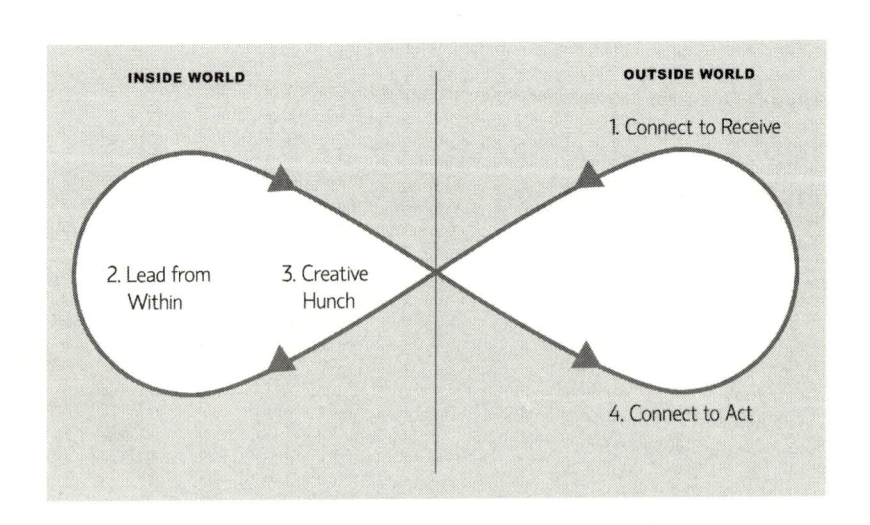

INSIDE WORLD | **OUTSIDE WORLD**

1. Connect to Receive

2. Lead from Within

3. Creative Hunch

4. Connect to Act

Connect to Receive

Your Talent creates significance for others, so connecting with the outside world is inherent to expressing your Talent. First, you will have to connect with the circumstances around you to identify opportunities that ask for your Talent. Your eye catches situations as if you have an antenna that receives a signal saying, "Here is something going on and you are the solution to it!" Then, you shift inwards, get a creative hunch, and act on it.

If you have identified your Talent, do you understand what gap your Talent solves? *Do you know what people and situations are your ultimate receivers?* Receivers are the people or situations that will benefit most from your Talent. Some examples:

- John is a *Simplifier*. He immediately signals situations where things get complicated. His ultimate receivers are people who are making things unnecessarily hard for themselves.
- Hella is an *Includer*. Her radar alerts her to people who feel left alone or situations where only parts of the context are highlighted.
- Sophia is a *Peacemaker*. Her eye catches how people relate to one another. She immediately sees when relationships are not harmonious.

It is important to train your antenna for situations and receivers to immediately identify them and to hone every sensor in your body to pick up the signals announcing that your Talent is needed.

Lead from Within

Again, I would like to repeat Frankl's quote, "Between stimulus and response there is a space. In that space is our power to choose our response. In our response lies our growth and our freedom." Because, right after you have spotted a situation that needs your Talent, you move into that space. It's *the* moment in which you can choose whether to be led by your dragons or your Talent.

At this point, your dragons start to scream: "Don't do it!" "Don't interfere!" "You are not good enough yet!" Or they send other discouraging messages, because your dragons sit right on top of your Talent. To access your Talent, you'll have to be completely aware and awake for what is happening and allow the dragons to take the backseat.

To have second thoughts is perfectly normal, because the situations or people who need you the most can also frustrate you the most. I was kind of devastated when I realized that the "ultimate" receiver for my Talent is a person who has a harsh dragon. These people can act scary. Of course, my dragons are alerted as well and want to come out and protect me. But I've learned along the way that the most important thing I can do is to shift inwards, breathe in, and simply remember my Talent and wait for a Talent hunch to arise. If you are ready to give way to your Talent, you can tell your inner dragon commentator, "I hear you, I respect you and still I have chosen not to listen to you right now."

Creative Hunch

Instead of impulsively reacting to situations, rely on your Talent and allow a creative hunch to kick in. Hunches are original ideas of how you add value in specific situations based on your natural response. Hunches are thoughts that pop up, ideas from the blue. Your Talent is amazingly creative—it creates all kinds of out-of-the-box interventions. It can be something you say or do. It could be an action to move something in the room, to make something for someone, to stand still next to a neighbor, to wink. It can be seemingly small this time and incredibly large the next time.

A Talent hunch is purely original and creative and completely new every time. Not one person or context is the same, so not one Talent intervention will be the same. It is so easy to conform to the situations and apply standard strategies learned in books or training programs, but our Talent hunches usually don't bother if they fit in—in fact, these hunches are the ones that have the potential to make you stand out. Following these hunches feels like ultimate freedom. It means a significant shift in the way you do your work and approach people.

Are you able to prepare a meeting and let your plan go because your antenna senses the actual situation and your hunch is different from your plan? Are you able to improvise, fueled by what your Talent whispers? Dear reader, living in alignment with our core isn't the comfortable choice.

Connect to Act

Nathan Sawaya[47], a Lego artist, puts it wonderfully, "Creative ideas are gifts, like windows that open for just a short time." Whether or not you are following up on those hunches makes all the difference. Hunches need instant follow-ups, otherwise the situation will change or your dragons will imply their judgments after all. Dare to dive into that window and add your original value.

It's all about timing. You can easily miss that window of opportunity. I remember a training I facilitated together with a co-trainer. We were doing an exercise where one of the participants was standing in the middle of the circle. She was having a hard time, but she was clearly on the verge of an important insight. That's when I got the hunch. In one flash, I knew I had to put my hands on her shoulders

---

[47] Nathan Sawaya, *The Art of the Brick: A Life in LEGO* (No Starch Press, 2014)

and stand behind her. But ... that would be crazy, right? So I didn't follow up with my natural response. I didn't miss the hunch, but I didn't dare act on it.

Guess what happened? A few seconds later, my co-trainer stood up and approached her in a different way, but that act gave the participant just enough courage to let it all out and let it go. A breakthrough. I am happy my co-trainer acted upon her hunch.

I am certain you will be able to experiment with your Talent in the real world following these steps: connect with your receivers, shift within, allow a creative hunch, and connect to act. Also, I am sure you will experience the freedom that comes with expressing your authenticity.

Finding ease with the uneasiness of Standing Out

So why isn't this the last page of the book? Why not leave it at this? My answer is simple. There is no getting away from the reality of most of our workplaces. The provocations within our current workplaces are tough and can easily disappoint us. Do we allow ourselves to let our Talent flow at defining moments, such as amid a presentation to the leadership of our organization? Do we allow ourselves to share our unique long-term perspective regardless of whether the rest of the room favors short-term gains? It's especially at times when we feel challenged that we start to feel uncomfortable. Do we allow ourselves to express our Talent when we start to feel uneasy? Before we know it, we forget about the value of our Talent and marinate in daily issues like we used to do.

Remember Kimberley's transformation? I decided to add three chapters to this book because of many similar stories like hers. Kimberley worked in an environment that didn't naturally invite her authenticity; worse, it discouraged her Talent to have any influence. Instead, she decided to dig a little deeper and developed courage in three areas. Dedicated practice enabled her to develop courage to *be led from within* (second step of Talent Expression), to *create* (third step of Talent Expression) and to *connect* (first and fourth step of Talent Expression). After a while, having practiced on these three levels, she noticed a certain ease with the uneasiness of bringing herself to work. She grew the courage to express her Talent.

Several philosophers, like Kierkegaard, Camus, and Sartre have proclaimed that courage is not the absence of despair. It is the capacity to move ahead in spite of despair. The next chapters of this book offer ways to prohibit your despair from standing in the way during defining moments where you can show real courage and leadership.

Rollo May wrote, "It is infinitely safer to know that the man at the top has his doubts, as you and I have ours, yet has the courage to move ahead in spite of these doubts. It means that this man remains flexible and is open to new learnings[51]."

How wonderful would it be if you find the courage to move ahead, despite your doubts?

Wearing our authenticity on the outside

Before you start reading the next three chapters, please reflect and ask yourself an important question:

Am I really willing to wear my authenticity on the outside?

You could keep your authenticity and Talent safely inside, like buried gold, occasionally showing your true colors in safe environments. If you haven't consciously decided, the steps afterward will not contain the moral fiber to keep going. If you start off sloppy, the results will also be sloppy. And no, it's not the easy road. A diamond is formed by consistent pressure over time. You really have to want to travel this road because it requires you to overcome some challenging personal roadblocks.

I hope you answered the above question with "yes," even it is a hesitant answer. I hope you start to grasp a sense of what your Talent entails and hope you can admit that your authentic Talent really is unique and can make a difference.

Also, I hope you start to experiment and begin digging out the gold to share what you have in store. It doesn't matter if you fail immensely while doing it or if you feel discouraged. All of your experiences, successes and failures, will help you understand the essence of the courage required to express oneself.

Pioneer on vulnerability research Brené Brown tells us in her books that the root of the word courage is cor—the Latin word for heart. And did you know that courage originally meant: to speak one's mind by telling all one's heart? To express from the heart is being brave and afraid at the same time. This original meaning of courage is aligned with what it feels like when we express our Talent. It seems like we turn ourselves inside out. We wear our Talent on the outside instead of our comfortable favorite dragon suit. In a way, we put our most precious and therefore, vulnerable, gold out there to be seen, and yes, to be that authentic feels uneasy when we express our Talent in an environment that doesn't necessarily invite us to show anything that derives from deep down.

There are no detailed maps

"So, how do I overcome that nasty feeling of awkwardness when I am doing something new, inspired by my Talent?" I hear you thinking. "Where are the maps or how-to guides to gain courage? Show me how I have to pull this 'Talent-thing' off." I am kindly warning you. If you are looking for predefined maps that tell you exactly what to do, you will leave disappointed. There aren't any. As I wrote earlier, each Talent is different, and your Talent is different in each situation. And above all, all of the real expertise is already inside of you. You are the pioneer, which means there is no map available.

The whole point of developing ease with the uneasiness is to not know exactly what is coming. When you are expressing your authentic Talent, you are walking on uncrossed land without a map, and that requires courage.

Let's be honest. Maps, theories, and models are simplified windows to deal with complex reality. They lead you on the way to your goal in a specific way, so as a guide, it's perfect. However, if we believe that there is just one way to look at reality, we are kidding ourselves. Before we know it, we fit into another belief system that controls our behaviors. Author Oriah writes, "Being unconsciously attached to our maps means we may ignore or not even see aspects of life that do not fit with our inner maps …" I also love the expression of Brené Brown, "You can't engineer an emotional, vulnerable, and courageous process into an easy, one-size-fits-all formula. Attempting to sell people an easy fix for pain is the worst kind of snake oil."

This book offers Authenticity Enablers

So, no maps with detailed routes. What this book does offer is different enablers to turn your inside out on your journey towards authenticity. Working in this field for many years, I have discovered that people who have learned to stand out with easiness have enabled themselves through dedicated practice on three areas: *Courage to Lead from within, the Courage to Create, and the Courage to Connect.* The next chapters of this book will introduce each area in depth. Each chapter, I will share two of the most important Authenticity Enablers.

These Authenticity Enablers offer you the possibility to integrate the insights into your daily life. It will require dedicated practice. Consider yourself to be working out by enhancing your Talent muscles page by page.

Wouldn't it be wonderful to shift within and learn how to handle your reactive tendencies? To enable yourself to rely on creative hunches to get the most impactful ideas to put your Talent into reality and make a difference? To enable yourself to act on them while staying connected with your receivers who benefit immensely from your added value? Even in the heat of the moment?

Serving delicious tea

My teacher, Birgitte Pastoor, explained the working of the Authenticity Enablers by using a down-to-earth metaphor. She said, "We are all like a tea kettle. We are meant to serve our most delicious tea." So the question is: Are we serving the world our full potential, our delicious tea, or are we serving dishwater?

The Courage to Lead from within is the Kettle handle and lid.
First, we need the handle to serve the tea. Without the handle, or the ability to handle ourselves, we aren't able to pour the delicious tea. We can only handle ourselves if we somehow practice to shift within without being distracted or seduced to react instantly. We have to handle situations with care, otherwise we drop the tea kettle and it's out of our hands. We have to practice, practice, and practice

some more to shift our focus inwards to consciously choose for our Talent instead of our dragons.

We also need to close the lid in order to boil our tea, otherwise, all will evaporate before you have the pleasure of serving it. Same with ourselves—this 24-hour society requires us to disconnect and close our "lids" regularly to stay centered and connected with ourselves. Before we know it, we have disconnected from ourselves and there will be nothing left to serve.

In the chapter *Courage to Lead from Within*, I will offer ways to center yourself to courageously choose your Talent instead of your dragons. This chapter will lead the way to staying connected with your authenticity instead of being disconnected by our mind-scattering frenetic society.

The Courage to Create is the Fire

We need the fire to heat the water. Did you ever get to taste half-boiled tea? We must use the fire to heat it all the way through. When we dare to really use our creative hunches we can transform the situation, independently if these hunches seem strange at first. The offspring of our Talent is creative and threatening to the status quo. To stand up and rearrange a meeting because we had a hunch about a better setup requires the courage to withstand strange looks from our colleagues. Not exactly what we people who like to fit in are after, right? So, do we allow all of our hunches to come through? Do we allow the creative fire to heat the water? Or do we let our Talent simmer over a low flame, and present our receivers with lukewarm water without a specific taste? We might not be used to trust our creative intuition. Or we might be afraid to get burned by the fire, just as we might be afraid to fail with our creative ideas.

The chapter *Courage to Create* will help you to cherish your curiosity to open up to seemingly strange creative Talent hunches. Also, this chapter exposes the vulnerability that comes with listening to your Talent hunches. If you want to trust your resilience and revitalize your workplace and beyond with new, original interventions, read on.

The Courage to Connect is the Spout

The way to serve the tea is through the spout. Our serving ability is our way of connecting our Talent with its receivers, the cups. When interacting with others, we usually create lots of noise on the line and this noise prohibits the clear flow of our Talent. So, is the spout allowing the delicious tea to flow or is it clogged in some way?

In the chapter *Courage to Connect,* I will elaborate on the most common roadblocks while interacting with a tough crowd. It requires courage to keep an open, compassionate mind instead of allowing frustration and judgments to take the lead. Understanding how you are influenced by relation dynamics leads to the full ownership of your Talent.

Let's start serving delicious tea! Surprise yourself with hunches that can make a difference, even if circumstances are challenging. Whether your intervention is seemingly small or whether you shake up foundations and revitalize the whole situation, be curious to walk into a forest without well-worn paths. To quote Vincent van Gogh, "Normality is a paved road. It is comfortable to walk, but no flowers grow." *We do want flowers, don't we?*

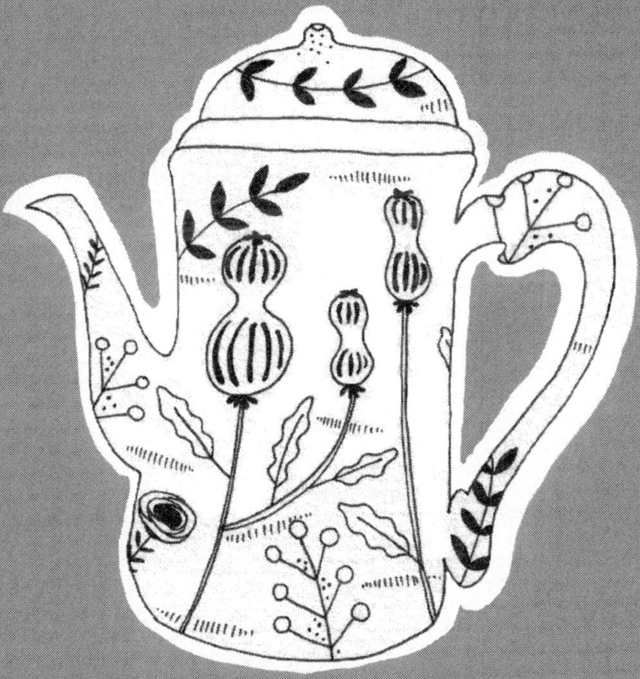

Each time we shift within, we are building a foundation from where we can perform in the heat of the moment.

NINE — THE COURAGE TO LEAD FROM WITHIN

Every time we are in a situation where we either fit in the mold or stand out in significance, we find ourselves at a crossroad. Do we choose to switch on our survival mode and try to fit in? Or do we have the courage to stand out and express our Talent? This crossroad is wonderfully illustrated by a tale:

An old Cherokee is teaching his grandson about life. "A fight is going on inside me," he said to the boy. "It is a terrible fight and it is between two wolves. One is evil—he is anger, envy, sorrow, regret, greed, arrogance, self-pity, guilt, resentment, inferiority, lies, false pride, superiority, and ego." He continues, "The other is good—he is joy, peace, love, hope, serenity, humility, kindness, creativity, generosity, truth, compassion, and faith. The same fight is going on inside you—and inside every other person, too."

The grandson thinks about it for a minute and then asks his grandfather, "Which wolf is going to win?"

The old Cherokee simply replies, "The one you feed."

Each time we decide to feed the evil wolf, we clear the path for our need to control our place in the outside world. Each time we feed this wolf, we pave the road towards its evilness, until the other road becomes less visible and it isn't a crossroad anymore. Then, we automatically let this evil wolf rule everything. You might recognize our dragons within this wolf.

Each time we decide to feed the good wolf, we clear our path inside. Each time we feed this good wolf, we pave the road towards our authenticity and our ability to use our Talent. Each time we pave this road, it becomes easier to walk, until the other road isn't more than a little side trail.

If we want to grow our imprint and we are fed up with our fitting in tendencies leading us to roads we don't really want to follow, all we have to do is start feeding the good wolf and paving the road within. That sounds easy, but it's not. Human beings are constantly being seduced to shift our focus outwards instead of looking inwards. In addition to this, we live in distracting times that can scatter our minds causing disconnection with ourselves.

Lastly, we may be afraid to uncover what is safely hidden in our darker corners. It requires real courage to choose to be led from within. It's not easy to shift inside, but with dedicated practice, we can certainly learn to. Each time we walk that path to feed the good wolf, our imprints pave it a little bit more. Enjoy the viewings from this path!

Staying in the lead of our seductions to turn outwards

We've already learned that our dragons pull us away from our vulnerable inner authenticity; after all, that is their role. They are guarding the entrance to our real selves. One way to keep us from entering is to seduce our attention to the outside world. Let's dive a little deeper into these seduction strategies.

Our dragons want us to find happiness quickly and easily. Happiness makes us feel good. We think, and are taught, that happiness is merely found in things and events outside of ourselves. According to the Buddhists, there are two sorts of happiness: Relative Happiness and Absolute Happiness:

- *Relative Happiness* comes from everything in our environment. Don't you feel happy when it's a sunny day? Or when you have a nice conversation with your friends? What about chocolate? Also, having a successful job where you get lots of compliments can make you happy. Our instant happy feelings rely strongly on things outside of ourselves.

- *Absolute Happiness* draws on our inner resources. We center ourselves, feel connected within ourselves, and establish a resilient state of life that is not easily swayed by outer influences. We are confident. Because we experience pure happiness inside, we are independent of outside stimuli. In this way, we can tune in with that happiness, regardless of our circumstances.

I remember experiencing glimpses of this inner happiness when I was participant of a training program fifteen years ago. I was sent on a five-hour walk by myself. At first, I was excited to leave so early in the morning, enjoying the sunrise and the freshness of the morning. "I should do this more often," I thought. But after 45 minutes, I started to get bored, not having anything or anyone to distract me. After 60 minutes, I already had eaten half the snacks they had given me. I became restless and was extremely aware of it because I wasn't distracted by other things.

At one point, I decided to sit on a log and do the meditation I had learned earlier that week. My mind still wandered like it was celebrating its restlessness, but at some point, my breathing helped to ease me. I felt the gentle breeze on my face. For the first time in a long time, I didn't need anything else other than just being in that moment. Sitting there with my eyes closed, breathing in and out, all was good. A sense of calm and serenity entered. I felt connected with myself, a state of being without worry, restlessness, and wanting everything to be different from what it was. It was all okay. By disconnecting myself from the distractions of the outside world, I was able to connect with my authentic being again. Since my early childhood, I hadn't experienced this "being in touch with myself."

After that moment, I opened my eyes and was blown away by the amazingness of my surroundings, as if a thin, invisible layer between me and the world had vanished. The brightness of colors, the beauty of the trees, the softness of the moss; my wonderment of early childhood had risen from a long sleep. Being connected with myself enabled me to also connect with my surroundings on a much deeper level.

This state of Absolute Happiness stayed with me for a while, but definitely needed maintenance. The challenge lies in the fact that we are constantly seduced by our Relative Happiness Hunt. Relative happiness is easy to find and fast to fulfill. We consume instant happiness, making us relatively happy using our five senses. We eat and we are fulfilled. We hear a compliment and we cheer up. We get a like on our social media and we feel special. In this fast-paced world, we are used to instant gratification; it is so easy to feed our "hunger" instantly.

Of course, this relative happiness is delicious food prepared by our dragons. They make us go after it so that we consume with pleasure and proudness and, slowly but surely, forget about our inner resources.

Everything we consume is quickly gone and we need more. Don't get me wrong—it's wonderful to eat a delicious meal, watch an exhilarating movie, or receive attention—it's our human nature as well. The problem is that we become addicted to everything that comes from outside and we begin to ignore what is inside. Our focus is constantly looking for where and how to get more. It's no wonder we don't want to turn inwards; we are on a mission to find extra input out there.

From a sleeping state of mind to an awake state of mind

When you listen carefully to the story of the two wolves, there are more than two entities involved. Not merely the evil wolf and the good wolf, but also the entity that decides which wolf to feed. That third entity is our awareness. When our awareness is asleep, automatism kicks in and the evil wolf is easily fed. When our awareness is wide awake, it reveals a choice: which wolf to feed right now?

You might remember the four states of mind described in Part I of this book? *The sleeping, the factual, the awake, and the absolute consciousness states of mind?* By constantly chasing Relative Happiness (see the table on top in the picture), we numb ourselves—feed the evil wolf—and we reside in the *sleeping state of mind.* We disconnect from ourselves and our

CHASING RELATIVE HAPPINESS

| Absolute State of Mind |
| Awake State of Mind |
| Actual State of Mind |
| SLEEPING STATE OF MIND
Dragons are in the lead |

CULTIVATING ABSOLUTE HAPPINESS

| ABSOLUTE STATE OF MIND |
| AWAKE STATE OF MIND
Talent is in the lead |
| Actual State of Mind |
| Sleeping State of Mind |

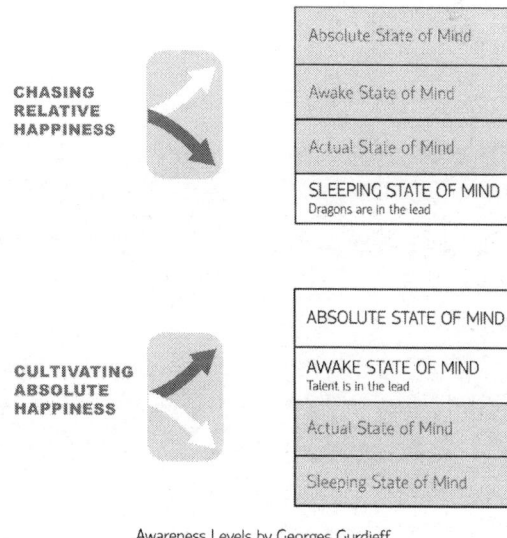

Awareness Levels by Georges Gurdjeff

inner resources. We therefore place dragons in the driver's seat and place our Talent in the backseat, or worse, in the trunk. When cultivating Absolute Happiness, we place our Talent in the lead (see the table in bottom in the picture). How can we get to *the awake state of mind*, where we feel confident enough to show up as ourselves and express our authentic Talent? How can we maneuver our ever-leaving awareness from outside triggers towards inside resources? How can we get a grip and let our own Talent lead to make a difference in defining moments, also when the going gets tough?

The answer to these questions is simple, although the benefits arise in the actual making it happen. We have to retrain our conditioned brains from shifting *outside* towards *inside*. We can start feeding the good wolf, which allows us to experience glimpses of this Absolute Happiness. We can only re-establish a connection with ourselves to feel confident about our Talent if we close ourselves for the outside world for a while. Therefore, the first way to practice expressing our Talent in challenging environments is:

AUTHENTICITY ENABLER #1: DISCONNECTING TO CONNECT

When we disconnect with everything outside and connect with ourselves for a moment, we can escape the Relative Happiness hunt. We can connect with our Talent instead of with our reactive tendencies.

The best tool for disconnecting to connect with ourselves is a very old one. It has already existed for over thousands of years. We can use *meditation* to establish a deep connection with ourselves. You may never have meditated or tried a few times after which you've decided this "pausing" was not meant for you. You may even get dizzy during all the conscious breathing like I used to get every time.

Yet, I would like to invite you to give it another chance in case you desire to express your Talent in challenging contexts. I know meditation used to be covered with new-age labels, but its essence is nothing more than closing our eyes for a moment to withdraw ourselves from everything that is happening. In corporate environments, I still sense taboos around meditation. Our mind's health is not something people easily talk about.

However, meditation will slowly but surely become mainstream in the Western world. The scientific proof is there. Over 3,000 scientific studies teach us about the benefits of meditation. Sara Lazar, a neuroscientist at Massachusetts General Hospital and Harvard Medical School, was one of the first to test the claims meditation and yoga experts made, by comparing MRI scans of two groups: a group of long-term meditators vs. a control group.

The long-term meditators appeared to have an increased amount of gray matter in the auditory and sensory parts of the brain, which means their ability to sense was stronger. They also found these long term-meditators had more gray matter in the frontal cortex, which means a better memory and executive decision-making. Maybe the most stunning result was that 50-year-old meditators had the same amount of gray matter as 25-year-olds. Usually the amount of gray matter decreases while aging.

This study might show the benefits of merely long-term meditators, but how about the advantages of meditation in case you've never tried meditation? Sara Lazar did a second study to research what happened with people who never meditated before and put them through an eight-week mindfulness-based stress reduction program. After scanning these people's brains and the control group's in MRIs, they found, again, remarkable changes. They found thickening in the regions responsible for a higher self-relevance, increased learning, cognition, memory and emotional regulation, perspective taking, empathy, and compassion.

Also, the amygdala, the fight or flight part of the brain which is important for anxiety, fear, and stress in general, got smaller in the group that went through the mindfulness-based stress reduction program.[48] People who meditate daily have altered their physiology in order to react less primarily and are better able to feed "the good wolf."

Corporate environments are desperately searching for their employees to have more agile mindsets, sharpened skills like attention, memory and emotional intelligence, all benefits from a regular meditation practice. Some of the organizations that already are offering mindfulness training include Google, Salesforce, Aetna, Goldman Sachs Group, Bank of America, and the U.S. Army. It's the evidence that even race cars need brakes.

What happens when we turn inwards for a while?

When we meditate, we stop and close our eyes and focus on our breathing. We metaphorically place a stick in a river. The outside world, the stream of water, is passing by. We usually flow with that stream automatically, if we are not drowning in the waves. When we meditate, we take a moment to stand still and hold on to the stick to observe the stream that surrounds us. Through our breathing, we

---

[48] Sara Lazar, Catherine Kerr, Rachel Wasserman and others, "Meditation experience is associated with increased cortical thickness" *Neuroreport* (2005)

become calmer and open to the present moment. From this place of calmness, the stick in the river, we get to really see what is going on. Or, like my eight-year-old son recently said after a ten-minute meditation, "It feels like I had a good sleep. Now, I feel really awake again."

There is more. Author of *Addicted to Love*[49], Jan Geurtz, explains how there are two different kinds of meditation. The first kind of meditation's main goal is to calm the mind. You learn how to ease your chaotic mind by "holding onto the stick," and it has a calming effect. In Sanskrit, this is called *Samatha*, which means "calming of the mind," but this is only half of the story.

In the second half of the story, we shift inwards. Each time we get to do this, we shift our mind from outward to inward, to see one's own real core. It's as if we turn ourselves 180 degrees and look at ourselves, our real selves. We get to experience a sense of abundance, as I experienced sitting on that log during my five-hour solo walk. Complicated things clear up. The addiction of needing the outside world for our recognition and confidence disappears as we realize that most of what we need is really inside. It's as if we tap into a well of unconditional love. Our judgments are erased by our sense of compassion. We arrive at the place of Absolute Happiness for a moment.

Each time we meditate, we pave the road towards our Talent. We get to establish the connection with ourselves and remember our worth. This allows us to tap into our own unique value. This practice lasts outside of our meditation; it allows us to connect with our surroundings authentically, as ourselves instead of pretending to be someone else. We tune in and turn on our Talent to approach things

---

49 Jan Geurtz, *Addicted to Love: The Path to Self-Acceptance and Happiness in Relationships* (Ambo|Anthos, 2016)

fresh. When we are working from within, we are in "flow," as psychologist and author Mihaly Csikszentmihalyi calls it, or "in our element," according to author and international speaker Sir Ken Robinson.

Sitting still?

"So, you want me to sit still and do nothing to achieve my goals?" my client Perry asked, frowning. It does feel kind of counterintuitive that if you want to make a difference in the outside world, you must first disconnect and do nothing. But when we want to rely on our own creativity and unique value, it is better to be still than to stay constantly busy. French philosopher and mathematician Blaise Pascal wrote in the mid-seventeenth century: "All of humanity's problems stem from man's inability to sit quietly in a room alone."

The Greeks already knew that sitting still was the catalyst to augment creativity. Did you know that the word *school* derives from Greek, meaning "free time"? According to ancient Greek philosophers, the most important task of a democratic leader was to enable free time. They noticed that when they sat still, their minds opened up for creativity. Contrastingly, tyrants often retain their power by keeping the crowd constantly busy.

During his leadership program, comedian and actor John Cleese showed a group of managers how the art of silence can lead to creativity. He asked them first to identify their biggest problematic challenge. He then placed them in front of a window and asked them to just think, stare, and do nothing else. After two hours of silence, none of the challenges were still considered as problematic.

Often, the most productive thing we can do is relax. We are very fortunate that we have the ability to—or are able to train ourselves to —sit still and clear our minds. By shutting our eyes and turning inwards, we don't turn our backs to the world. On the contrary, we are able to see this world more clearly.

However, it requires dedication to place commitment on the center of your own being. Athletes already realize this in their bones; they practice to arrive in the zone. Phil Jackson, coach of top athletes including the NBA's Michael Jordan and Kobe Bryant, taught them how to be present in order to foresee the game while in the game and to rely on their inner strengths instead of falling back in old habits. He also taught them how to reset themselves after failure. They meditate to keep an open mind and become mentally strong and resilient.

A routine enables us to build a strong inner foundation

The biggest challenge of this Authenticity Enabler *Disconnect to Connect* is to create a routine of shifting inwards. We need dedicated practice to withstand our reactive tendencies to turn outwards. If we want to be able to perform in the heat of the moment, we need to be able to rely on our meditation muscles to keep feeding the good wolf. Consider yourself a firefighter practicing the same drill over and over so you'll be ready to tackle the toughest blaze.

Each time we practice meditation, we pave the road until we can't miss the turn anymore. Once this muscle gets stronger, we are able to shift inwards and let our Talent drive instead of our dragons. It allows us to express our Talent in situations that normally would make us nervous. This ability allows us to be authentic in situations that don't invite us to be authentic. And you know why?

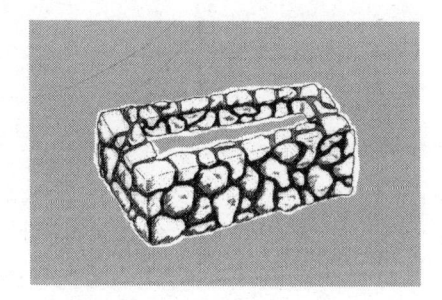

Because each time we practice, we add one block to our foundation. Each time we meditate, we are building a foundation that will hold us when the storm hits. Therefore, each attempt to meditate makes a difference.

Once Perry was convinced of the benefits of meditation, he managed to sit down for 15 minutes at least three times a week. Despite his still-wandering mind, he enjoyed the brief moments of intense relaxation. The relief he experienced during these meditation moments informed him about how exhausted he really felt. He observed his tendencies of trying really hard. His whole life was filled with trying hard. He tried to be a good son, a good father, a good husband, a good friend, a good colleague. He saw himself taking up the enormous weight of responsibilities, like he was Atlas carrying the whole world on his shoulders.

Every time he sat down and connected with himself, his confidence grew and his need for approval shrank. His face brightened as if the shadows of the weight literally vanished. After some weeks of dedicated practice, the first signs of a better connection with himself emerged. He realized how his tendency to fish for compliments faded. He even stopped meddling in disagreements between his brother and father. He quit his tennis team after already thinking about it for two years. His cravings to belong to everything outside himself diminished bit by bit. He became more comfortable with the risk of standing alone. He reminded me of Maya Angelou's quote: "You only are free when you realize you belong no place— you belong every place—no place at all." Once he felt connected with himself, he sailed on the trust coming from building that inner fort. His colleagues noticed his expanded leadership presence during meetings. He was able to act autonomously and authentically, consciously resisting the exhausting need to carry the responsibilities of the whole world by himself.

But how do you create a routine to keep building that inner foundation? Trust me, over the past 20 years, I've come up with my share of excuses to not meditate: *I'm too tired; I really need my sleep in the morning; meditating and young children are no combination; I will do it after I check my emails,* etc. At one point, I realized that I needed help establishing a routine. So I registered for weekly yoga classes taught by teachers who also facilitate meditations. I checked in with friends who also meditated regularly so we could remind each other. Registering for a virtual pilgrimage led by Britt B Steele[50], yoga teacher, hit the nail on the head. I managed to sit still, meditate and do yoga for 108 days (okay, almost 108 days) in a row.

The ball is in your court now. If you want to be sure to tune in with your Talent and stand out confidently, start a meditation routine today. It's totally okay to allow yourself to be helped to create a dedicated practice. It is helpful to reside in some sort of "container" that reminds and inspires you to stick to your routine. Hurray for the millions of challenges online! Hurray for meditation teachers who teach weekly mindfulness courses to ensure you with a regular practice. Hurray for apps like *Calm, Headspace,* or *Smiling Mind.* We simply need this routine to be able to live inside this human mind that is easily seduced.

Suggested routine

To guide you through the woods of hundreds of different kinds of meditations, I would like to share my favorite two meditations at least. I've tried lots of them in the past 20 years, but I always return to my regulars. The first takes me only 10 seconds and the second one about 20 minutes.

---

[50] Britt B Steele, *Pilgrim, Living your Yoga Every Single Day* (Deva Daaru, 2016)

- *10-second meditation:* During this "power" mini-meditation, the single thing I do is focus on my breathing. I inhale for four seconds and exhale for six seconds. During the exhale, I release my neck and shoulders and breathe towards my feet.

Our breathing is one of the most amazing aspects of our body. Not only does the constant and effortless flow of oxygen and carbon dioxide keep us alive, our breathing is the most efficient tool to influence our nervous system. A long in- and exhale can instantly redirect the attention from outside to inside. Within 10 seconds, we can relax our mind and reconnect with our inner self instead of being led by our dragons—move from your sleeping state of mind into an awake one. We can do this at any time without anyone noticing.

I recently met someone who installed an app on his Apple Watch that vibrates each hour to remind him to breathe consciously for a few seconds. This brilliant reminder enables him to be an eye in the storm, which can be a challenge for an executive within a Fortune 100 multinational, like him. While everyone else is caught up in heated discussions, he breathes a few seconds, reconnects with himself, and is able to come up with a clear and fresh approach. Simple and effective.

- *20-minute meditation:* Once I read Jan Geurtz's explanation of the difference between the calming meditations and the ones that invite you to build your inner foundation, I understood why I have an absolute soft spot for the *Latifa meditation.* The Latifa is an ancient Sufi meditation practice. It was first described by a Sufi mystic in the thirteenth century, but probably it's much older. The word "latif" has different meanings, but all of them have something to do with being subtle. This meditation guides you through seven human qualities: Acknowledgment, Desire, Hope, Trust, Letting Go/

Surrendering, Love and Will. Each quality touches the subtle core of being human and reconnects us with ourselves and strengthens the relationship with the refinement within us.

What I like about this meditation is the fact that it isn't about stoically putting up with unsatisfactory situations (as I experienced in some other meditation methods), but instead we use the energy and creativity of the "Absolute Happiness" to transform those unsatisfactory situations.

This might sound pretty serious and laborious, but honestly, this meditation is easily accessible for everyone—even for those with no meditation experience or those who usually find it difficult to meditate. It used to be secret for a long time, only passed on by speech because of its immense power. About twenty years ago, Michael Derkse, author and Sufi teacher, brought this meditation to Europe and altered it for western use. Feel free to download a guided version of the Latifa meditation on my website.

Did you know that the best moment to meditate is early in the morning? A good start is half the battle. I sense an immense difference when I start the day being silent for a while, reconnecting with myself. Those 20 minutes build the foundation for the whole day. And each day you can start over. Yoga teacher Britt B Steele encouraged me so often when my warm bed was much more inviting than getting up to meditate by saying: "Just rise, sit, and wake up later."

Staying in the lead of your fear to turn inwards

Meditating and allowing the silence into our lives to fuel our Talent sounds lovely and very spiritual, but taking a pause can feel like a waste of time. We close our eyes and after the first conscious breath, our to-do list creeps into our mind. Random things like dinner plans, logistic schedules, or a presentation prep keep fighting for our attention. It's almost as if our mind is screaming, "You really think you can sit still and do nothing? That's not how you're going to reach your goals!"

If your impatience keeps bothering you after you've read the last pages and have tried at least seven times, something else might be going on. You might be apprehensive to dive within yourself because you're unsure of what you'll be discovering. Your mind might be warning you to keep that lid closed; perhaps you are secretly afraid that undesired emotions will show up. Being silent and alone can feel like floating disconnected from safe land with nothing to hold on to.

What you'll find when silent

Becoming more aware and living from the awake state of mind can give you bliss, but as wonderful it can be, it also can be frustrating. And you are not the only one. An article in Science shares the research of Professor Wilson and his team. They reported 11 studies where participants preferred to administer electric shocks to themselves instead of being left alone for six to 15 minutes in a room with nothing to do except think.[51] Why is thinking and sitting still for a few minutes worse than electric shocks?

By being silent and turning inwards, we start to feel more. We might have numbed and distracted ourselves for a long time because it was just easier that way or things were too painful. But honoring our desires to feel more alive and feel happiness, we also encounter darker emotions. Those can hurt and frustrate. They can well up in our chest, throat, or heart and make our head feel incredibly heavy or

---

[51] Timothy D. Wilson, David A. Reinhard, Erin C. Westgate, "Just think: The challenges of the disengaged mind," in *Science*, Volume 345, Issue 6192 (2014).

tired. I love how author Amy Jen Sy puts it: "Mindfulness is not all gloom and doom, nor is it all sunshine and flowers."[52] Undigested past negative emotions still anchored in your body can arise while sitting still. They rise up to be dealt with, which is usually what we need to do.

Have you heard of JP Sears? He is a comedian who calls himself a spiritual healer. His videos about the spiritual journey madness are hilarious. He mocks the earnestness you repeatedly find in spiritual teachings. As funny as he is, he actually shares wise insights.

JP Sears refers to e-motions in two ways.
- *Evil motions:* We usually perceive emotions as something we have to get rid as fast as possible. We perceive e-motions as evil motions that we try to avoid instantaneously. We surround ourselves with a shield and lock all difficult emotions out. We bite the bullet. This is how we dissociate ourselves from our bodies and turn into numb robots. The irony of it all is that despite our efforts to ignore these feelings and emotions, they are still there. Even more so, they can become toxic for our system. If we don't work through them, our bodily functions will try to work through them, sometimes in harmful ways.
- *Energy in motion:* If we start perceiving these e-motions as energy in motion, we will then recognize these feelings and emotions are worth setting them in motion, at least when we feel brave enough to. The Latin derivative "emotere" literally means "energy in motion." We need to digest them, according to JP Sears. We need to unclog our emotional digestive system. Wrestling with emotions is like a detergent for letting them go.

---

[52] Amy Jen Su, "If Mindfulness Makes You Uncomfortable, It's Working" *Harvard Business Review* (2015)

This process can be challenging, and seeking professional help is a sign of strength instead of a sign of weakness.

Staying in the lead of our distracted minds

We can now work anywhere, anytime, even while commuting, traveling on a plane, or waiting for someone. Even our private restroom moment can be a time to check our smartphone. We are distracted more than ever, and every moment of downtime is squeezed out of our lives. Without those in-between moments, it's hard for our senses to calm down. An abundance of outside digital stimuli is overloading everyone. There is hardly any time left to retreat within, to reconnect with ourselves.

No wonder our Talent is easily neglected. The continuous stream of demands makes us run with no end in sight. Without a compass to navigate, we can easily become disoriented and lost. When we are running ourselves to death to meet deadlines, we react to circumstances instead of creating new or better circumstances using our Talent. So, what to do to "stay awake" amid the chaos of phones, emails, meetings and family rushes?

Believe me, I struggle big time with lots of technology-related distractions. I even wrote a goodbye letter to my iPhone because I was so fed up with it taking my time. A few weeks later, the same iPhone crept back into my life, not staying farther away than an arm's length. I know I am not the only one. In fact, nowadays the average

US consumer spends five hours a day on their mobile device. That is a 20 percent increase in time spent compared to 2015.[53]

Nevertheless, people all over the world are trying to win back the lead by organizing off-line Shabbats, retreats, and initiatives like Onedayoffline and the National Day of Unplugging. I organized my own 40-day digital detox. I was curious how my smartphone actually was influencing my daily life. I was allowed to check once a day to keep up with emails and social media. You know what? Some days it went well; other days I cheated like a true addict, easily coming up with multiple excuses. In the end, I discovered a very important difference between time ruled by my phone and time ruled by me.

What normally would be an in-between moment now ruled by my phone was something I described as "hazy." This is what I wrote down at the time:

I am looking for that one email. My eyes are scrolling down hundreds of emails with hundreds of different subjects. After ten minutes, I give up. I check my WhatsApp. One new message from a group-app. LinkedIn, how about that? Interesting posts of interesting people—will I ever be able to read it all? Maybe later, probably never. Too much information. Back to my email, nothing new. My eyes focus on the red circle: three new Facebook messenger messages. Maybe that'll be interesting? My eyes go square, itchy. The doorbell rings. Is it already 3 p.m.? I wish I had more time.

---

[53] Simon Khalaf and Lali Kesiraju, "U.S. Consumers Time-Spent on Mobile Crosses 5 Hours a Day" *Flurry* (2017)

In-between times where I ruled my time myself, I described as "free." These sentences tell my experiences without being captured within the digital world:

My head leans backwards. I exhale. I look around without really having to see anything. My eyes soften. A flying bird catches my eye. I follow her until she flies out of sight turning bends. I hear sounds from outside, near and far. My feet are cold. My breathing is deeper and relaxed. What I see outside touches me. This is soothing. The incredible palette of colors, movements, and resourcefulness. Suddenly, an idea for my client arises, out of nowhere.

Really, we live in exciting times as technology solves complex problems. However, sometimes, I feel as if we are living in a science fiction movie and our consciousness has been captured by technology to make us numb and unaware of what is really going on. This 40-day experiment taught me how I was captured by my phone. It also taught me what happens when I am in charge of my own time. My mind relaxes itself, my wonderment grows, and my connectedness with myself and the world around me expands. My Talent is so much more in the foreground. Who on earth would choose a constraining look over an open and free look at the world?

Who is your friend—Chronos or Kairos?

In the movie *Wonder Woman*[54], Diana sees a man from the outside world for the first time after living her entire life on a secluded island. Seeing his watch, she wonders what his wristband stands for. After his explanation about time, she asks, "So you let that thing determine what you are doing?"

---

[54] *Wonder Woman* by Warner Bros Pictures (2017)

In our society, after the industrial revolution in the eighteenth century, we have let *Chronos*, the personification of (clock) time, run our lives. Many people, for example, health care professionals, are judged (and paid) by the numbers of actions they can perform in a preset period. Whether or not they put quality into those actions often remains unnoticed. Time—especially the lack of it—becomes our enemy, a thing "we have to beat." We try to do too much in too little time. Our opportunities to tune in with ourselves become scarce with the effect of our efficiency-dragons ruling our world.

Wonder Woman/Diana leads her life by understanding another meaning of time, namely *Kairos*. Kairos is another ancient Greek word for time, but it focuses on the opportune time for doing certain things. In fact, she comes alive when the clocks are silenced. When we let Kairos take over measurable time, Chronos, we enable igniting and inspiring moments that make our lives worthwhile to take place. In those Kairos moments, we sort of place ourselves above the clock's time. We know Kairos has taken over when we are concentrated, in a flow, such as reading a book, listening to an engaging presentation, or gazing into the eyes of a loved one. It's like a wonderful piece of music. Unlike a metronome's constant rhythm, enjoyable music isn't static, it slows down and speeds up; the variety makes it interesting and worthwhile.

Philosopher Joke Hermsen[55] describes how we lose track of time in Kairos moments. We submerge into what we are doing in such a way that we *are*. In this submersion into ourselves while experiencing a different aspect of time, a direct door opens to ourselves. In these moments, we are led from within instead of by the clock. These moments are incredible opportunities to gain unexpected insights and

---

55 Joke J. Hermsen, *Stil de Tijd*, (De Arbeiderspers, 2015)

hunches and a great time for our Talents to come out. Our Talent is encouraged by inspiration rather than pressure.

What is your relationship with time? Is Chronos your thing? Is time an instrument to measure if something can be accomplished? Do your appointments rule you? We are used to the fact that the pace *outside* ourselves dominates our rhythm. Due to technology and the way our society is organized, we are inclined to keep up with a frenetic pace. If you want to fit in, certainly, it's smart to tune in with the organization's rhythm. The downside is that the organization's rhythm will never slow down. It keeps going and makes us run like hamsters on a wheel, being slaves to (a lack of) time. I can tell you one thing, Kairos is nowhere to be found near that hamster wheel.

If we want to make use of our Talent, we need to familiarize ourselves with Kairos. The main step we can take is to be led by our own rhythm instead of someone else's. It requires at least a sense of it. In Kairos moments, we are not harnessed in the pressure of efficiency; we allow ourselves to be inspired and tap into new possibilities. That leads to our second route to enabling ourselves to express our Talent in challenging environments:

AUTHENTICITY ENABLER #2: OWNING OUR TIME, OTHERWISE IT'LL OWN US

I remember when I first acknowledged Kairos after multiple years of running flat out, trying to squeeze in more activities within an hour.

That day, I had to finish a proposal for an important client, but, not surprisingly, I had too much on my plate. I had facilitated an early morning meeting in a city far away after a late night preparing for that presentation. When I drove home after having experienced the high during the meeting's success, I actually felt tired and empty. I had no idea how I would be able to create an inspiring proposal after feeling so drained.

Then I got a hunch. What if I returned home first to take a bath and relax for 30 minutes before continuing my work for the day? Luckily, I sensed what I needed because after that bath I was able to create an incredible proposal within an hour. After that bath, I really was effective. I experienced an enormous amount of flow. I realized we are not robots. We are not programmable to constantly perform on a high level from nine to five, or more. We are humans, affected by a multitude of things. Our impact is so much bigger when we tune in with our energy and use what is available at what time. Sometimes, we need less sleep; sometimes, we need more sleep. Sometimes, we are creative; sometimes, all we want to do is listen. Sometimes, we are inspired; sometimes, we are not. Our society needs an enormous amount of creative solutions, so why do we still think the clock is the one that dominates?

Everything in nature has its own pace. We are a part of nature, so why would we fit into the strict and standard program of the workday? Fitting in with other people's rhythm is fine and doable, but not all the time. Sometimes, we have to catch our own breaths or use our inspiration when we feel we have plenty. There is a right moment for everything.

Manage your energy instead of your time

I dare you to try something radical. Pick a day within the next two weeks. The goal of this day is to turn it upside down. Place yourself ahead of your planned activities in your agenda. Instead of being dragged from meeting to meeting, ask yourself how you would design your day? What is very important for you to make a difference? How can you allow your Talent to shine through? What is important for you to show up 100 percent?

It might involve canceling a few less important meetings. Really, some meetings do fine without you. It might involve shortening a one-on-one meeting (which in most cases leads to higher quality). It might involve adding an activity that inspires you, such as listening to music, walking in the park, or enjoying your favorite dessert. It might be an activity to recharge your battery, like a short breathing meditation or taking a relaxing shower.

Be creative in your new day design. Don't let standard schedules rule. Instead, allow Kairos to take a peek. Does it mean rising at 5 a.m. to start your day with meditation or a workout? Wonderful. Do you choose an activity that soothes you instead of exhausting you? Organize it. The important game changer here is that you ask yourself: what do I really need this day to show up as myself in order to make a difference?

Include your time after coming home as well. When you enter the front door after work, ask yourself: What do I really need the first few minutes? What is my internal clock telling me? Is it walking the dog outside to get some air? Is it some quiet time with a hot tea? Is it chatting with my family members?

Once you start doing this, you will notice that it is anything but a selfish act. In fact, it allows you to share your value with others much better. Your level of concentration and creativity improves, which allows you to do things much faster and better. You enable yourself to include your authentic self instead of being on autopilot. Start to manage your energy and inspiration instead of your time; you'll soon notice the difference.

Birds make great
sky-circles of their
freedom.
How do they learn
to fly?
*They fall, fall,
and falling,
they are given wings.*

- Rumi

TEN — THE COURAGE TO CREATE

"How do you facilitate your employees to make a difference and express their individual Talent?" I asked a human resources (HR) representative of a Fortune 100 company. She began to speak enthusiastically about programs for their creative designers. After ten minutes of hearing about wonderful initiatives for creatives, I started to wonder, "What about the people working in operational roles?"

She explained how in every function the window in which you can be disruptive or creative is different. "Each business unit has a different take on that. When you are a designer, your specific role is to be creative and unique, to think outside of the box. You have to come up with something new and not yet defined, so there is a lot of room for your specific authentic approach. A person in Operations needs to execute following strict standard rules. Disruptive ideas might harm the strictness of internal processes."

A person in Operations might not get the same freedom as a designer, but if an organization merely expects that their employees perform within the current standards, they are likely to miss out on their unique value. After a while, they will stop producing creative ideas for improvement. More and more, they will be led by rational thoughts and will act on their autopilot, not realizing they're missing out on their creative hunches. Their full potential stays locked inside the box.

The standard processes within an Operations environment might ask for Talents that seem less creative at first sight. However, imagine what could happen if you discover that your team member flourishes when he creates *Order in Chaos*? Wouldn't he be the first one to ask to prevent weaknesses in the system? And what if you discover a colleague's natural Talent is to bring a *Holistic point of view*? Wouldn't you invite her to create a strategy on how to approach a fast-changing complex retail landscape? And that logistic center employee who is the best *Motivator* when everyone is tired; wouldn't it be wonderful if he is allowed to spread his energy around the clock on busy shipping days? What a difference would that make?

Unfortunately, many organizations don't yet recognize the importance of unleashing the uniqueness of their employees. Their programs and procedures are designed to control complexity. They are focused on standards, which require uniformity, predictability, and orderliness. They discard the value of authenticity and their employees' ability to make real differences.

But our Talent is extremely intelligent and creative. Our creative hunches do not reckon with existing norms and behaviors. The ideas that spring from our creative hunches do not aim to fit in, so they inherently let you stand out in significance. Our Talent's goal is to add value and make a *difference*—and to make a difference, our hunches provide us with ideas on how we can approach situations and circumstances *differently*. These ideas are usually different from what our automatic pilot is used to, different from what our surroundings are used to (from us), and maybe even different from our role specifics.

In environments that naturally do not welcome our authenticity and originality, we tend to fit in and put a lid on our creative hunches. Originality is not invited, so why allow those hunches to keep appearing? If our comfort zone had a voice, it would say, "Most of what your Talent inspires the world with is strange and scary. Don't bother." Strange, because it's different from the status quo. Scary, because we would have to show up as ourselves, which feels vulnerable and, in some cases, *is* vulnerable.

If our stretch zone—the zone in which we challenge ourselves and where we are able to learn the most—could speak, it would kindly invite us to experience the abundance of our creativity, even in discouraging environments. We will have to find the courage to open ourselves up to it and to our intuitive hunches, despite them being strange and scary. Finding the courage to create, we can amaze ourselves and our surroundings with what a difference our Talent makes.

Isn't it wonderful that we possess the amazing ability to create? I want to emphasize that when I speak of creating, I don't mean concrete things only. Talent interventions also include ideas, gestures, acts or anything that is new, original, and different to you and/or the outside world. Anything that is different from the status quo. Anything your auto-pilot wouldn't do.

The following intermezzo shares Paul's story. He steps with one foot outside of his comfortable space and stretches himself despite his doubts. Read and learn how everyone in this story is able to add value using their Talent, no matter if the intervention seems small, huge or strange.

INTERMEZZO : Paul's Talent story

Paul is a team leader within the new business development department of a large software company specializing in children's education. Lately, he has realized his attempts to change internal mindsets are failing. The clock is ticking. He knows a large part of their traditional business soon will be extinct. Already, new competitors are taking over their current target groups. The company is struggling, and so is he.

His initial enthusiasm to be part of changing the game is subtly fading away. Is he fading away himself? The rat race of serial meetings has taken its toll. Does he really have to attend every meeting he is invited to? Does he really need to deliver every report anyone asks for? Honestly, he is fed up with all that extra work. Aside from it costing a lot of energy, he doesn't have the feeling he is adding much value. He is exhausted and has no energy left to change even his own mindset. In a way, he blends in with the people of his organization who he is trying to prepare for the future. He is too caught up with daily business to even think about future changes.

During his last one-on-one meeting, his manager said she felt as if he didn't make use of his full potential. She had the feeling he had more in store, but he wasn't showing it yet. What did she mean? Is his tendency to be friends with everyone in the company making him lose himself? Was she referring to his initial drive to move things forward? No wonder he can't make the impact he wants. Where is his adventurous mind? His heart jumps thinking of all the adventures he ignited in his earlier years. His wife recently reminded him of the amount of energy he used to bring into the room with his exciting initiatives. Those were the days when he felt free to play. What if he could reconnect with that Adventurer mindset and bring that to the office? What would happen?

In the middle of that night, he wakes up. What if he steps forward to take the lead in the introduction of the latest new product, a platform that has the potential to include children in schools all over the world to teach each other? What if he is able to create one big adventure for the whole organization? What if he approaches the introduction differently this time and gets rid of the standard procedures contaminating every ounce of enthusiasm for new products like they usually do? What if he can ignite the hearts of every salesperson out there in such a way that they will run the extra mile to show this new platform to new and existing clients?

He is curious what he could be capable of. His creativity is flowing already. His curiosity appears to be the antidote for his judgments. His curiosity creates space and gives way to creative ideas that night. That morning, he will ask his manager if he can take the lead.

But, stop ... is this really what he should be doing? He is already exhausted, right? Maybe he should just relax for a bit. All this adventurism was nice when he was young, but now, it is serious business. He shouldn't be playing around. His (lack of) energy won't sustain all the criticism he will likely receive from his colleagues for his wild ideas. Stop playing, start working. He grabs his pillow and tries to fall back to sleep.

The next morning at ten, he has to hurry to the team meeting. His manager comes in at the same time, smiling, recognizing his rush and asking him to first get drinks for everyone. Heading over to the coffee machine, he slows down his pace and remembers his idea stream from that night. Will he just take this leap? Somehow, he trusts his idea stream and feels almost curious to see what this event could initiate.

After he puts the drinks on the table, he sits down and sees his manager looking around the room. She is curious if anyone has any ideas for the upcoming event to introduce the new platform. After the first ideas come to the table, Paul's frustration begins to rise when the usual standard setups are presented. Suddenly, he does it. He raises his hand and says semi-confidently, "Let me do it. I have had some great ideas. I know that we can turn this event into something people will never forget. This new product deserves special attention."

His heart is pounding. His hands fumble with his pen. Paul lifts his head. His colleagues stare at him. He feels like he is standing at a crossroad. He can either choose to back down and downsize his new responsibility while he still can or he can grasp this new opportunity and choose to go (and grow) on this adventurous road. Is this what people mean by the difference between the head and the heart? His heart is pounding and feels bigger than normal, allowing an almost silent encouraging whisper to come through, "It's okay, Paul. This is a good thing." His head feels heavy and full, as if it is about to create a short circuit. He almost can't think straight.

Amid this rage between head and heart, he realizes he wants to use his full potential. Will it mean that he should take new roads? While looking across the room, he feels small and insecure. Despite these feelings, he somehow decides to go forward and give way to the encouraging whisper. Fortunately, his manager acknowledges his step forward and supports him to make a good start.

The next couple of nights, Paul hardly can sleep. A mix of insecure thoughts and creative hunches keep him awake.

He knows he can't create an unforgettable event by himself. He instantly knows who to invite to join the team. Becky always makes a difference in connecting with all the different stakeholders within the other business units.

Laura has always been like an eye in the storm of chaotic work situations. He is sure she will be able to create ease in uneasy situations. He also includes Glen, who always has been like a lighthouse to him. He somehow knows what the next step should be when others don't have a clue what to do.

Paul gets another hunch. He never likes long projects because internal politics often interfere. He enjoys the intensity a short-term project creates. It reminds him of taking an adventurous journey. He decides to organize this new platform introduction event in just two weeks. They officially will start a month from now. He isn't sure how everyone's agendas can make it work, but making the suggestion won't hurt anyone.

Surprisingly, to him, his team instantly accepts his invitation, not only because of his enthusiasm, but also because they each feel seen in their abilities to make a difference. They resonate with the adventurous vibe Paul is showing lately. Paul's enthusiasm is contagious.

Those two weeks are a festival full of wild ideas, smart thinking, and preparations. Inspired by Paul's adventurous approach, Laura suggests creating a home base in one of the small rooms in the back of their office. Glen develops an insightful plan on the wall of their work space to oversee how things progress. Becky works on involving stakeholders in a way they don't want to ignore her. In fact, they are charmed with her way of communicating. Paul's energy of creating adventurous ideas flourishes and energizes the whole group. After many diverging and converging brainstorm sessions, they come up with quite the adventurous idea for the event. They will invite the children of several stakeholders within the company to enter the platform, use it, and share their experiences. They already have received positive replies from the involved families.

Also, Paul makes sure everyone is aware of each other's Talents and dragons. Before the two weeks start, they dedicate one and a half days to identifying their primary tendencies that potentially could influence this project, as well as their individual authentic Talents. Allocating tasks becomes so much easier once everyone knows how the other person can make a difference. And they know they can rely on each other. Being open about their dragons initially feels awkward, but it appears to be helpful in stressful situations. It creates an easy opening to give feedback before things got out of hand.

For example, that moment when Paul backs off and freezes when an executive enters their project room. Laura immediately recognizes his dragon, steps up, and makes sure they can present what they are working on. Afterwards, Paul understands that his dragons were at play and thanks Laura for taking over his responsibility.

A couple of hours before the event, Paul suddenly has a though: "What if we turn things upside down and use the stage for the participants? That way, they might feel in charge, which was exactly the point of this new software program." He isn't sure. Is this over the top, or is this actually helping to make a significant difference?

This last hunch appears to be the dot on the "i." The participants are surprised by this unusual setting; Paul immediately catches their attention. The whole event is a huge success. The attendance and participation of the children is refreshing and unexpected. One of the parents tells Paul's team afterwards, "Suddenly, I was reminded of our company's purpose; we make products for 'our' children. This instantly made me reconnect with a certain engagement I had lost for a long time."

The attendants are impressed. The adventure during the event inspires them to take their company's future more seriously. They decide to invest a larger amount of money and resources towards making a change.

Familiarizing yourself with strange hunches that challenge conventional ways

Our routines and paved paths only provide an illusionary safety net, but at least they are familiar to us. Paul craved releasing that hidden adventurous part of himself to let it roam around freely and introduce new ideas and stand out, but he had significant hesitations.

The dance between our need to fit in and do what is expected of us, and our desire to stand out and make a difference is delicate. Who is in the lead? Our desire to show up and change the current realities? Or our desire to feel safe and swim with the tide? Remember the tea kettle metaphor I introduced? Do we let our Talent simmer over a low flame and only present our receivers with lukewarm water? Or do we dare to fire up the heat despite our hesitations and allow ourselves to be inspired with creative Talent interventions to transform the situation?

Imagine a situation at work that catches your eye. It might be a conflict in your team, a project with a dead end, or a colleague who's afraid to present. Do you ignore this situation? Do you follow the usual path? Or do you allow your Talent to respond and listen to the whispers and hunches, like Paul did? If you choose the latter, you have to trust your creativity to kick in with an intuitive idea that arises from within, a feeling in one's bones.

What are these strange Talent hunches?

Arriving at the deeper levels of facilitating personal development training programs usually involves someone saying, "This is too vague for me." You might also agree that sentences involving your creative hunches, your inner voice, or your inner compass do sound fuzzy. After all, what do they actually mean? Trusting your inner hunches sounds abstract because you cannot actually see these hunches. You cannot grasp them like numbers on a spreadsheet. There are no best practices available since they are original and new in this moment. However, I don't believe that the vagueness disclaims the existence of it. There are more things in this life we cannot see that actually do exist. The moon and the stars still exist during the day, although we don't get to see them. And we did not see temperature rising until we had instruments to measure that phenomenon. That remained invisible, yet it didn't mean that warmth or frost didn't exist before the thermometer.

These unmeasurable Talent hunches rise from our intuition. They hold an important well of knowledge within ourselves we do not see. Film director Stephen Spielberg refers to intuitive hunches as whispers and that's exactly what they are, "I've always said to my kids, the hardest thing to listen to—your human personal intuition—always whispers; it never shouts. So, every day, you have to be ready to hear this whisper; let it tickle your heart."

According to the authors of *Mastering Leadership*,[32] intuition is "a practice of opening to a deeper knowing, a higher sensory perception that says, '*stay with this*' or '*do this now*'. Or '*This is who you are, what you stand for, what you need to move toward is this ...*'." Intuitive ideas spring forth from unknown parts of ourselves; that's why they are so authentic and original. These ideas are not shared all over the Internet, written in books, or taught in school (yet). They are new and original. That is why intuition is "the source of breakthrough insight, wisdom, and transformative vision. The source of most great innovative advances." Intuition is the source of our Talent—the source of standing out in significance.

A better understanding helps us to better recognize our creative intuitive hunches. To demystify what a gut feeling, hunch or intuition actually means, this summary by Professor of Organizational Behavior at the University of Surrey Eugene Sadler-Smith[56] might help. Intuitive hunches:

- arrive rapidly, without deliberative rational thought
- difficult to articulate verbally
- based on a broad constellation of prior learning and past experiences
- accompanied by a feeling of confidence or certitude
- affectively charged

Although intuitive Talent hunches can be very strong, we tend to easily ignore them because they come from a place we never were taught to trust. So, the next time when you notice that "moment of truth" hunch rising in your mind or that gut feeling in your bones, realize it might be strong and original material with the potential to revitalize your surroundings.

Destroying the status quo is the birthplace of all transformation

Creative Talent hunches are wonderful and usually highly appreciated, but their strangeness also ruins the status quo in a way. My professor handed me a book when I was doing research at the Delft University of Technology in 2000. "It is old, but still valid," he said. It was called *The Courage to Create* by Rollo May.[57]

Back then, I was already intrigued by the book's title and content, and even more than seventeen years later, I still think he makes a lot of sense. May wrote: "We live in a world that has become mechanized

---

[56] Eugene Sadler-Smith, "Intuition, neuroscience, decision making and learning" *Triarchy Press* (2006)

[57] Rollo May, *Courage to Create*, (New York: Norton, 1975)

to an amazingly high degree. Mechanization requires uniformity, predictability, and orderliness." He also wrote about our fear for "potentialities that surge up from deeper mental wells." They might not fit. The creativity of the spirit threatens the structure and presuppositions of our rational, orderly society. "Irrational urges are bound by their nature to be a threat to our rationality," and that's the main reason we tend to ignore strange creative hunches to rise to the surface. If we want to stand out and make a difference by doing things differently, we will have to understand that "every act of creation is first of all an act of destruction," as Picasso used to say. And that's okay. I know it sounds strange to say, but destroying the status quo using our Talent is the birthplace of transformation.

Supernovas are probably the best illustrators of this phenomenon of destruction enabling creation. Supernovas, the explosions of stars, generate all the chemical elements, including carbon and nitrogen, that are used to make everything in our universe. "Life might not be possible without vast, mysterious, and ongoing transformation" according to the authors of *Journey of the Universe*.[58] When we stand out, creating new scenarios using our Talent, we destroy "the way we are used to do things around here," and at the same time, we produce fertile ground for positive change.

Sometimes, our Talent may be welcome, but environments that are averse to risk actually prevent creativity from happening because they want to maintain the existing order. Isn't that the highest risk of all? In an ever-changing world, organizations need to enable themselves to destroy the "box" in order to grow and transform into a better place.

---

[58] B. Swimme and M.E. Tucker, *Journey of the Universe* (Yale University Press, 2011)

What about yourself? Did your tendencies to fit in slowly fade your creative hunches? You might have built your own internal organization full of fixed mindsets, rules, and dogmas in your mind that lock up all your creativity. Aren't you curious what your abundant creativity has in store for you when you escape that prison? Imagine what the "potentialities that surge up from deeper mental wells" might mean for you and others. You *can* escape this prison and surprise yourself and others.

The next Authenticity Enabler helps us to create a Curiosity Vortex to ignite our creative Talent hunches to come from our deeper mental wells.

AUTHENTICITY ENABLER #3: ESCAPING FIXED REALITY BOXES BY UNLEASHING CURIOSITY

Paul, the team leader in the intermezzo in the beginning of this chapter, experienced how his curiosity disabled his judgments to let the fragile hunches eventually appear to the surface. He nearly didn't escape from his own fixed reality box and thought he had such a busy agenda that he wouldn't have time to make a difference.

He was trapped in a box of daily routines before he realized he could also bend the rules and habits to make a difference. (picture by Jan de Dreu).

To open the lid to where our creative hunches come from, we can train our curiosity to invite them to reappear. The same curiosity will also prevent your hunches from being immediately crunched by our judgments and tendencies to fit in. Think of brainstorm sessions where we separate divergence (creating ideas) from convergence (selecting ideas)—we simply postpone our judgment for a while.

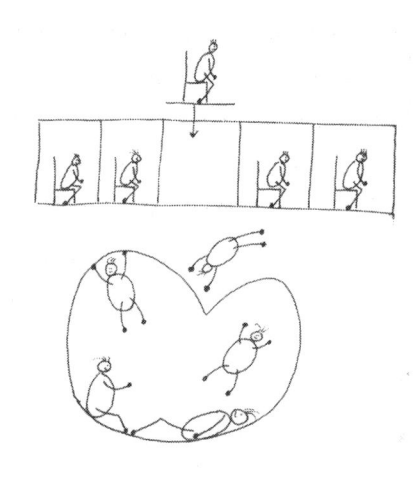

Curiosity energizes and encourages us to find out more before our judgment system kicks in. The reason lies within our brain's wanting system. The research of doctor in psychology Matthias Gruber[59] of the Center or Neuroscience identified what areas are activated when people are curious. These areas appeared to be within our dopaminic circuit, also known as the brain's wanting system. So curiosity energizes us via the brain's wanting system, making us want more and more. Asking curious questions allows you to create a Curiosity Vortex. That vortex allows you to escape fitting in a box, for a while. It allows you to think through "what-if?" scenarios, allowing the boundaries of the box to fade bit by bit. Maybe these hunches aren't as strange as they once seemed?

---

[59] M.J. Gruber, B.D. Gelman, and C. Ranganath. "States of curiosity modulate hippocampus-dependent learning via the dopaminergic circuit," in *Neuron*, Volume 84, Issue 2 (2014)

Instead of letting a conforming world make us feel paralyzed and reside in apathy, why don't we start to experiment and start wondering what our Talent ignites? Let's put this third Authenticity Enabler into practice and challenge our fixed realities by researching the following areas and raising as many questions as you can think of. You might be amazed by what freedom your Talent creates if you give your authenticity priority over your current way of thinking and acting.

Questioning your way towards freedom

Events on an average day
During your next meeting, presentation, or any casual encounter with colleagues, ask yourself a number of questions:
- What do I really think of the setup of this meeting/presentation/conversation?
- How does it make me act, feel, react?
- What effects does this current form have on other people? How do they act, feel, react to it?
- When I put my Talent first, how would I revitalize this event? Start by being astonished by your mind's creations. Chuckle to yourself when a new hunch reaches the surface. You may not be doing anything with them yet, just be incredibly curious.

Your functional role
We are bigger than our role. However, we usually identify ourselves so much with our functional role that we get stuck in it. We overrule all originality and stick to what is the official way it's always been done—how our peers are performing. However, our functional role is merely a vehicle for our Talent to make a difference, helped by our experience, knowledge, and other skills.

We can make a difference challenging the set boundaries, not because we want to be rebellious, but because a new set of boundaries enables us to improve our value. Jobs and functional roles are not molds for us to fit into as perfectly as we can. They are just vehicles to serve people to add value.

Colleen Barrett, executive vice president of Southwest Airlines from 1990 to 2001, understood this principle and allowed employees to be themselves by focusing on "what" needed to be established instead of the "how." For example, flight attendants were encouraged to deliver the legally required safety announcement in their own style and with humor. If we are not restricted in the "how," we can infuse our acts with authenticity. This philosophy made Southwest, at the time, a top industry performer in terms of passenger volume, profitability, customer satisfaction, and turnover.

So invite your curiosity to turn your thinking upside down:
- What do I consider my role to be myself (if I don't stick to official boundaries my organization is setting)?
- For whom do I actually work, meaning for whom will my work make a difference? Lots of times, we are bound by thinking we work for our manager, but we really work for our clients, customers, students or patients.
- What would my function profile sound like if I could rewrite it? What should be part of it to energize me?
- If my Talent were superior to my functional role, what would I do to make a difference?

What you've been taught
Sometimes fixed ideas about how we should do something keep us within boundaries that don't allow us to use our Talent. If all school teachers stuck exactly to the curriculum and taught exactly the same teaching strategies, it would soon turn into a boring school day.

We can challenge our fixed mindset by being curious. What it would look like if we added our own unique spice to the mix, just as William did when he finished an extensive coaching course. One of the main teachings was to be cautious of giving advice. That's right, the coach's main goal is to facilitate clients to create new insights themselves. However, he identified his Talent as *Wise Council*, which meant he gets incredibly wise hunches/insights for his clients. But when should he follow his Talent, and when should he follow his coaching teachings? If he sticks to his teachings, his hunches will die down. Like William, you can ask yourself:

- When do I let 'official rules' prohibit my natural way of intervening?
- What would a work trajectory look like if it was in my style?
- How would I be able to incorporate my Talent hunches as well as staying loyal to what I have been taught?
- When should I act on hunches; when is it fine not to?

What you think you "are" or "should be"
In most cases our own fixed self-images are also pretty strong obstacles for our creative Talent hunches to abundantly flow. If we are attached to a self-image of let's say, a tough businesswoman, but our Talent is *Listener,* any hunches that involve tenderness will have a hard time rising to the surface.

Be honest and think about what self-images you hold on to and how your self-image conflicts with the essence of your Talent:

- What self-images do I hold onto about myself? Am I trying to be the expert or an academic? Or do I consider myself to be "just" a mom?
- How does this affect the use of my authentic Talent?
- What would happen if I erased those images?

- If I have an open mind about myself, how can I surprise myself and others with my Talent?

Let the words of psychoanalyst and philosopher Louise von Salome inspire your curiosity: "What if the so-called inviolable bounds drawn by convention turn out to be nothing else but innocuous chalk lines." Yes, you'll feel uneasy if you choose unconventional ways. You'll feel uneasy crossing boundaries set by others or by yourself. But what if those boundaries turn out to be drawn with chalk? Why not start to feel at ease with your uneasiness and play with those flexible frontiers? Let's dare that difference.

Familiarizing yourself with scary hunches that make us feel vulnerable

Once our curiosity shows us in what kind of box we reside in and challenges our boundaries, we can step outside of this comfortable box and let our Talent lead. However, we still feel scared to act on Talent interventions. Our Talent doesn't take our insecurities into account. Genuine Talent interventions require us to show up as ourselves and wear our authentic cores inside out. Living without a mask to hide behind can feel like driving without your seatbelt. Acting on our Talent can feel vulnerable, especially in non-encouraging environments.

Damian identifies his Talent as *Future Perspective*. Will he allow hunches that inspire him to share his opinion in a room full of vice presidents? Fanny is an *Eye in the Storm*. When she recognizes a chaotic mind, her Talent produces innovative ways to ease the other person. Does she allow unorthodox ideas like connecting through eye contact just a tad longer than usual? Or will she be scared away by the intimacy that comes with that?

Damian's and Fanny's dragons scream: "This is too awkward," "this doesn't work around here," or "you are not good enough yet." Their Talents don't scream; they just provide intuitive hunches. But what if Damian and Fanny keep ignoring those hunches because they're too scared? Their hunches will start fading away.

Turning our insides to the outside feels vulnerable

"It's incredibly nice and adventurous if you stop thinking you're not good enough." So true, right, this quote by writer Arold Langeveld? Also challenging. Somewhere along our way, almost all of us get our creative confidence damaged. Our memories of when that happened might not all be as clear as my client Zackary. He desired coaching because he was unable to set up his own business successfully. He easily got distracted and discouraged. We soon discovered that he had lost his creative confidence, meaning he self-sabotaged all his serious attempts towards making a difference. In one of our sessions, we discovered the core of his creative insecurity.

In high school, he was selected to become a member of the student newspaper. He and a friend got to make the first edition of that year all by themselves, since the seniors were occupied with tests. They worked hard and put all their energy into covering interesting stories. Although the paper wasn't as thick as normal editions, he and his friend were proud of the result. When the pallet full of newly printed newspapers arrived at school, he saw the president of the student newspaper council picking up a fresh one. Curious to his thoughts, Zackary awaited his feedback. The only thing the president said was, "This is so thin, it looks like toilet paper."

You can imagine how this relatively small incident had a huge effect on Zackary's creative confidence. Being an impressionable teenager, he wasn't able to see things in perspective in an adult way. Also, his negative feelings got to grow undisturbed, because he didn't dare to share this experience with anyone for years. This event subconsciously took its toll up to the present time. Deep down, he still thought every new project would turn into toilet paper. To prohibit anyone from hurting him, he unintentionally sabotaged his creative projects along the road. He constantly distracted himself with social media, news, other people's needs, and whatever he thought needs his direct attention. Insecure thoughts paralyzed his creativity in a way that the end results weren't as successful as they could have been. Also, he assured that he'd better go in other directions, which result in him rarely finishing creative projects to a point he could really present them to the outside world.

We've all been hurt in some degree for putting ourselves out there at some point. When we are creating from within, like we do when acting from our Talent, our confidence starts to shake. When we put our heart into something and that gets crushed, like in Zackary's case by a single remark, it feels like our whole reason of being gets crushed. When we stand out, we turn the inside outside. We release our precious treasure, full of potential, and wear it on the outside, which feels incredibly vulnerable. We bring what's building up inside our heart on the outside without knowing if it will succeed. This uncertainty hurts our ego-loving dragons. These dragons want us to compete, want us to win, or at the very least, want us to fit in. And they thrive on compliments. So, to show up as our authentic self without guarding it and kindly resisting the protection of our dragons requires courage.

As our culture's competitive pull is so strong, our focus on winning overrules almost everything. We shouldn't show up vulnerable; no, we should show up using our armor and weapons, presenting our "best" selves all the time. What's the price we pay not doing that? Are we really losers when we show up as real people? Better an "oops" than a "what if," right?

The main character in Joel Dicker's book *The Truth About the Harry Quebert Affair*[60] has trapped himself in a self-constructed perfect world. In high school, he chooses running instead of football because he knows he'll have a better shot at excelling on the track. Does he really like to run? Not really. Throughout his life, he continually focuses on circumstances that allow him to win easily. He's successful, yet unfulfilled, until his mentor confronts him with the truth: "You will only embrace life if you dare to fall."

If we constantly protect ourselves from falling and live a caged life within secure boundaries, we hide from receiving pain and disappointment. But that same cage also prevents us from connecting with our passion and joy. It's like living our adult lives as toddlers with over-protective parents. If we don't dare to fall, we don't dare to fly.

It's as if we've been caged birds all this time. Suddenly, after having familiarized ourselves with strange hunches, we realize our cage has fewer and wider bars. We can roam around free, except we haven't learned how to fly yet. Our fear of falling keeps us sitting still. Our fear of failing while expressing our authentic Talent in challenging environments keeps us "safe" within our cage.

---

[60] Joel Dicker *The Truth About the Harry Quebert Affair* (Penguin Books, 2014)

It's only once we leave our cage that we can show up completely. It's only if we dare to fall that we actually dare to use our full potential. It's time we discover what it means to learn to fly, which brings us to our next support for expressing our Talent in challenging environments:

AUTHENTICITY ENABLER #4: DARING TO FALL IN ORDER TO FLY

Let's take a look at the different questions we ask ourselves when learning how to fly, aka learning to turn our authentic Talent to the outside:

- *Learning the value of vulnerability:* Is the pain of falling worth the attempt of flying? In our case, what is the value of being vulnerable?
- *Releasing tension:* How do we fly when we are still afraid? Do we put too much weight on our wings? In our case, what are the effects of too much tension trying to stay in control?
- *Trusting our resilience:* If we fall, what enables us to get back up? In our case, what does it mean to be resilient? What do we gain in case we fall?
- *Improving our flight skills by making test flights:* Making test flights is the only way we will experience what freedom actually means. In our case, what do we gain from making small leaps?
- *Becoming our own reference point:* Do we fly to receive an applause? In our case, how does that influence our course and how can we fly towards our own goals?

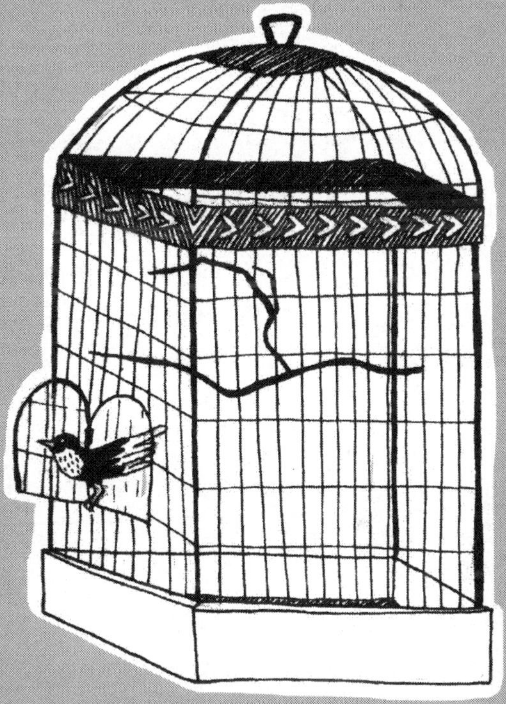

Learning the value of vulnerability

I meet people who think that being vulnerable means expressing all emotions on the spot. They would never cry in front of their boss in case they feel emotional, and I get that. But vulnerability primarily means that we acknowledge all emotions. It means that we acknowledge that we are strong *and* flawed, like every human being. We sometimes think we actually want to be robots, logical and unemotional, but we are not. Robots are tools; we are not. Being vulnerable means that we realize we can fail. "Vulnus" literally means wound; being vulnerable means "getting out there risking an attack."

Being real is what we mean when we talk about vulnerability in the context of personal and leadership development. Being real means that we acknowledge we are human beings with strengths and flaws. It also means that we are not trying to hide flaws, which is incredibly brave. Did you ever notice that someone who tries to hide their vulnerability appears much weaker than someone who dares to show up as a real human being? Think of people who are overcompensating their insecurity by a loud and strong voice compared to people who still make eye contact despite their red cheeks. Think of the singer with the imperfect voice that resonates on an emotional level.

This difference between being real and trying to be perfect was never so clear as when I invited leaders to kick off a development training program. The participants hung on every word from leaders who were open and who allowed the participants to take a peek into their own vulnerabilities. People are more interested in the actual story than the manufactured one.

Lady Gaga's remark is true: "If you don't have any shadows, you are not in the light." I remember playing a game with friends when we were teenagers. We had to describe each other's strengths and flaws. When it was my turn to be "evaluated," they couldn't come up with clear weaknesses, but they also struggled to come up with clear strengths. They didn't say it, but afterwards I realized that withholding so much of what was inside of me made me kind of bland. I was so busy trying to avoid criticism that I became almost invisible. I was clearly following Aristotle's advice when he wrote: "To avoid criticism, say nothing, do nothing, be nothing."

According to Brené Brown's research, vulnerability is the birthplace of love, joy, empathy, and creativity. I instantly understand this when discussions with my husband turn from nasty to friendly. The moment one of us is ready to admit what's really going on inside or says something honest, the armor lowers and we are immediately able to reconnect. We can only experience true freedom if we escape our safe cage.

Brown also explains how vulnerability is the source of innovation and change. You can't really make a difference without risk or uncertainty. If you've created a work culture where vulnerability is accepted and even valued, you also have created a culture where making a difference is encouraged. Project Aristotle[61] is a research project at Google to identify what teams need to do to be effective. They studied over 180 teams, and the data indicated that psychological safety, more than anything else, was critical to making a team work effectively. Feeling safe allows teams to take risks and explore unchartered areas.

Project Aristotle has taught Google that no one wants to put on a "work mask" when they get to the office—they'd much rather show up as themselves, real human beings, vulnerable and all. To be fully present at work, to feel psychologically safe, people must know that

---

[61] Charles Duhigg, "What Google Learned From Its Quest to Build the Perfect Team" *New York Times* (2016)

they can be free enough to share the things that scare them without fear of recriminations. And be free from judgments in order to experiment with creative ideas instead of feeling limited by the focus on efficiency all the time. Google realized people have to dare to fall in order to fly.

Releasing tension

Our fear of failing awakens the control freak within each of us. Our desire to control everything is one of the ultimate killers for authenticity. *"This meeting has to go perfectly,"* ; *"I have to appear as strong as I can";* or *"My client has to accept my proposal."* The tension fires up. We live in the illusion that if we keep control, we will fly, but it is exactly the other way around. Imagine a bird trying to fly with stiff wings. While we try to hide our vulnerabilities because of our fears of not being perfect or accepted the way we are, we turn into "stone." Rumi invites us to "be crumbled":

Very little grows on jagged rock.
Be ground. Be crumbled,
so wildflowers will come up
where you are.

You have been stony for too many years.
Try something different.

In avoiding every uncovering of our flaws and insecurities, we avoid every feeling and emotion. We shut ourselves off from real connections, because they might hurt us. We stop bringing authentic parts to work because we are not fully sure they'll work. The attempt to control everything makes us reside in our mental capacities. But hunches that revitalize our surroundings will not appear in this controlled tense mental mind.

To be able to receive creative Talent hunches requires letting go of too much control. We have to allow creativity and imagination to kick in, but our control dragons certainly avoid any non-proven methods. Einstein discussed this with a friend from Princeton: "The mind needs the relaxation of inner controls—needs to be freed in reverie or daydreaming, for unaccustomed ideas to emerge." My teacher Jan de Dreu gave me the same advice. He repeatedly said, "Lean back, don't try too hard." *Be your Talent, don't act like one.*

Imagine you have identified your Talent as *Listener*, and you're trying really hard to be a perfect listener. You'll perfectly follow all the theoretical rules of listening, but before you know it, you'll fit into a new box instead of relying on your true authenticity and allowing your original Talent to intervene. The whole point of leaning back and enduring your insecurities and tendencies to be perfect is to allow your intuition to enter the stage, roam free, and trust your creativity to do its job.

How do we fly when we are still afraid? How do we not put too much weight on our wings? My client Jenny immediately came up with the answers to these questions. The expression of her Talent made her think of sailing and how you learn to catch the wind to allow your boat to advance. If we pull the ropes too tight, the wind flows past the sail and we lose power. If we let go of the sail too much, the wind doesn't catch our sail, which makes the boat also slow down. Somewhere in between there is a sweet spot where we can sail at maximum power. It's the same with expressing our Talent. Somewhere in between too much control and a "letting it all go" mentality is where we will receive those creative Talent hunches. Staying relaxed, while being alert and focused.

Trusting our resilience—learning what we might learn while falling

This summer I taught my children how to do backflips into the swimming pool. Intrigued by this challenge, they were standing with their back towards the water, constantly twisting their heads assessing the situation. They were ready to jump, but their faces expressed the "will I or won't I" look. Eventually, they seemed to trust their ability to bounce back from a sour back just one bit more than they feared the situation. At the moment that realization kicked in, they jumped. Courageous acts might feel as if we are jumping into a swimming pool backwards not knowing when, how, or even if we'll reach the water.

One important element of daring to show up authentically and, therefore, daring to be vulnerable, is the trust that we will bounce back if we fail. When young children are learning how to walk, they keep getting up to try again. No matter how many times they fall, they don't quit. Without this try-and fail-marathon, they would never learn how to walk, run, climb, swim, sing, dance, speak, or read. The fact that we trust our abilities to "rise strong," as Brené Brown calls it, to get back up after disappointment, helps us to do it again. And again and again. This ability that helps us be courageous is called resilience. *Are you able to get back in the ring after being punched, or is the fight over?*

After hearing the personal stories of hundreds of training participants about resilience, I observed an interesting quality that people maintain who showed resilience. No matter how painful their stories were, they kept an open mind. They all showed a sense of curiosity and a desire to grow personally through their painful experiences. Their growth mindset enabled them to keep asking themselves questions. Why did it happen? How did it happen? What was my part? What can I learn from it? What can I improve next time? Instead of feeling like they were victims of events and were imprisoned within a fixed mindset, for the most part, they were genuine learners. In a sense, they gained after failing.

Developmental psychologist Emmy Werner[62] published the results of a 32-year longitudinal project. She followed a group of 698 children in Kauai, Hawaii, from before birth through to their third decade of life. The most important outcome of her research showed the difference between resilient children and children who were less resilient. The resilient children had an "internal locus of control." Those children believed that they, and not their circumstances, affected their achievements. They kept learning despite their disappointments, and they believed that they, themselves, were in control how they dealt with future events. They saw themselves as the orchestrators instead of as victims. That didn't mean they thought they could control everything in life, but they believed they could control their own reaction after setbacks. In fact, on a scale that measured loci of control, these children scored more than two standard deviations away from the standardization group.

Attitude really affects our whole outlook on the world. Do you ever hear yourself saying, "Why does this always happen to me?" or "I will never ever learn to do this!" Doesn't that feel kind of paralyzing to you? What if you start asking, "What does this setback tell me?"

---

[62] Maria Konnikova, "How People Learn to Become Resilient," *The New Yorker* (2016)

And start wondering, "What is a small first step I can take to improve things?"

Leonard Cohen eloquently and honestly sang, "Forget the perfect offering. There is a crack, a crack in everything. That's how the light gets in," in "Anthem[63]." Instead of hiding your imperfections behind a mask, start facing things. When I have trouble accepting this true fact of life, I read this poem by Rumi daily for one week.

The Guest House

This being human is a guest house.
Every morning a new arrival.

A joy, a depression, a meanness,
some momentary awareness comes as an unexpected visitor.

Welcome and entertain them all!
Even if they are a crowd of sorrows,
who violently sweep your house empty of its furniture,
still, treat each guest honorably.

He may be clearing you out for some new delight.
The dark thought, the shame, the malice.
Meet them at the door laughing and invite them in.

Be grateful for whatever comes.
Because each has been sent as a guide from beyond.

---

[63] Leonard Cohen, *Anthem* (1992)

I wish we all would remind ourselves of our resilience in courageous moments. We only need *just* enough to stand out and shine. I wish we would all stand out like beautiful flowers blossoming without holding back. I wish we would all show our colorful and vulnerable petals proudly, ready to receive sunlight, rain, and admiration. If only we could trust our roots to ensure our stability, should we get crushed.

Improving our flight skills by making test flights

This may be your opportunity to begin a special project in which you will stand out in significance. Are you ready to learn how to elevate your "leadership presence" with your newly gained confidence? Surprise yourself and others with what happens when you are led by your Talent.

A widely-held myth suggests that creative geniuses rarely fail. Yet according to Professor Dean Keith Simonton of the University of California, the opposite is actually true: creative geniuses, from artists like Mozart to scientists like Darwin, are quite prolific when it comes to failure—they just don't let that stop them. His research found that creative people simply do more experiments. They take more test runs. Their ultimate "strokes of genius" don't come about because they succeed more often than other people—they just do more, period. They take more shots at the goal. And yes, test flights aren't without bruises. But if we want more success, we have to be prepared to shrug off more failure.

It's exhausting to keep ignoring our true selves, because we use false energy and eventually our flames and passions burn out. So why not practice instead of pretending? Start with small leaps. Because if we never leap, we'll never know what it is to fly.

When I realized that my Talent had a lot to do with tenderness, two female colleagues came to mind. They were the tough women who made bold choices and appeared strong. This tenderness didn't seem to match with them, at least not in my view. They symbolized the ultimate reasons why I wasn't really inclined to do anything with my new discovered Talent. Figuratively speaking, I saw them slapping back immediately when confronted with any tenderness. For a long time, I wasn't ready to show up, take ownership of my Talent, and receive their judgments in any form. I had placed these colleagues above myself, and I felt like a weak bird without wings until I had a moment of clarity and I asked one of them to meet me. I aspired to be a trainer in their newly established business unit that involved profound change. Somehow, I had found courage to ask for a role.

I still remember where we sat in our company restaurant when I explained why I wanted to work for her clients. She was listening, but at one point she said, "I am afraid you are not firm enough for our clients." My cheeks turned red, and I stumbled trying to find a prompt answer, but then I surprised myself by saying, "I realize I come across as vulnerable because of my tenderness, but is that really the same as a lack of firmness?" And then I added, "I think it would actually benefit your clients to see my vulnerability and at the same time see that I keep standing in the arena. Isn't that exactly what we want to teach our clients?"

Boom! She stumbled and somewhat agreed to my words. However, she kept repeating her previous message. I never got to work with her, but that encounter felt incredibly liberating. I had escaped the illusionary birdcage and was actually flying.

This leap of courage made me ready for more. That's how taking small or big leaps work. Leaps position you in the stretch zone and slowly transform it into your comfort zone. The more test flights you run, the more they carve a successful path in your brain and the more you start trusting. Or, like Rumi wrote:

Birds make great sky-circles of their freedom. How do they learn it? They fall, fall, and falling, they are given wings.

Do you think you will need a little push to "jump backwards into the swimming pool"? Consider Benjamin Mee's quote, author of *We Bought a Zoo*[64], to be your little push, "You know, sometimes all you need is twenty seconds of insane courage. Just literally twenty seconds of just embarrassing bravery. And I promise you, something great will come of it."

Start with small leaps, no problem. As long as you just start playing with your Talent abundantly. Step by step, you will regain your Creative Confidence and enable yourself to express your authentic Talent in any situation that requires *you*. Even if your acts of Talent seem strange. Even if your acts of Talent seem scary.

Becoming our own reference point

Beware of one important thing, though. The whole "trust ourselves" issue is a big challenge for us *fitting-inners* and we tend to give the lead to someone else to decide whether our test flight performance was great or not. We haven't really developed our own sense of judgment. I recommend that we develop our own points of reference instead of leaving that up to others to decide. It is time to regain our autonomy.

---

[64] Benjamin Mee, *We Bought a Zoo*, (Weinstein Books, 2008)

At the end of my second year of coaching and training, I had to prepare a challenging exercise for my own group. It was a real test flight within a safe environment. It was only 30 minutes, but being a perfectionist, I thought it had to be the greatest moment ever. I remember that Sunday morning as if it was yesterday. I had it all figured out and prepared the notes, the music and the space. Everyone entered the room, including my teacher. I managed my fears and facilitated the group according plan.

My intention set for this exercise seemed to have worked, looking at their faces when they left the room. But my tension wasn't gone because I was about to have a follow-up conversation with my teacher. Did she like it? Was it enough? Was it up to standards? We sat down and she began asking two questions. What did I do well? What could I have done better? The eager student in me answered these questions perfectly. Finally, she said, "Okay … thank you. I'll see you later today." What?! Wasn't she supposed to give me an evaluation?

I remained seated for a few minutes after she left until it slowly began to dawn on me. My conditioned student mind yearned for appreciation from my teacher, because that's what teachers do, right? But the lesson she taught me was to merely make me aware of the fact that I could be my own reference point in evaluating my test flight. Brilliant. She knew me so well to know that I, myself, would be the most critical of all the people in the room. I, myself, would be able to evaluate my performance. For years, I had placed the answer to "am I worth it?" in someone else's hands.

It's so refreshing to become our own reference points. All our lives we have accepted being judged by others. We are so used to teachers grading us and bosses evaluating us. And we learn to crave other people's approval so much that we jump through many different hoops to please them. It's exhausting. In an effort to please others, we lose our confidence and our ability to assess ourselves. We walk from side to side because we don't trust ourselves to walk ahead.

It's time to regain the leads. No one knows this terrain of your Talent better than you. You'll gain trust and self-confidence as soon as you stop fishing for compliments. You are the real expert, so just ask yourself two questions:
1. What did I do well?
2. What could I have done better?

The answers serve one purpose: to learn. So, it's important that you just give one answer to each question instead of a whole list. Just one, because who will remember a whole list, in moments when it really matters?

Well, dear reader, prepare for take-off. Just sit back, relax, come up with amazing Talent interventions, and enjoy the flight.

Standing out by expressing our Talent is the opposite of being egocentric.

It's all about serving others, about having a positive impact—so everyone wins.

I don't use my Talent to score;
I use my Talent to touch.

ELEVEN — THE COURAGE TO CONNECT

Wholehearted leadership in its core

This entire book primarily focuses on you. That might seem a bit self-centered, as if the rest of the world doesn't count. Actually, the opposite is true. Being able to identify and express your Talent simply requires lots of navel-gazing and self-reflection. This leaves you with worthwhile insights, but this self-reflection is not the primary purpose at all. The primary reason is to enable you to create positive effects for the world around you. Really, the juiciest fruit of personal growth is the ability to contribute. Your Talent is your unique way of creating meaning and significance for others.

While we were busy with fitting in, most of our connections were designed to provide us with recognition, attention, and applause. We interacted with others to make us feel better about ourselves. We gave what we thought was our best in order to get something in return. In a way, we were parasites, because without the other, we could hardly exist. We used the outside world to fix our inner problems.

While standing out, our connections are designed to give our best. We interact to express what's bursting to come out to create value for someone else. There is no ego involved. This is wholehearted leadership in its core. We don't do it because we receive a medal. And indeed, you might not receive a shining medal, some of your Talent interventions might even remain unnoticed, but you *will* leave a legacy. Our natural response simply wants to add value, and we tap from our abundant source of creativity to find the right way to do it. We are giving instead of receiving.

Our interaction with others is an essential part of expressing our Talent. We connect with the people and situations whose problem are a trigger for our Talent to express itself. Talent interventions probably are the most unique and authentic interventions we have ever shared or will share. Zooming in on how we relate with the people that receive our Talent is worthwhile because, ultimately, we strive for a purely authentic, high-quality connection without any roadblocks from our side.

This chapter zooms into two parts of the connection we establish during Talent moments:

- *The receiving part:* How can we observe our receivers with an open mind?
- *The expressing part:* How can we share our Talent with our receivers without holding back?

You might understand how these two parts are different from each other. It is like the inhale and the exhale. Do you have any idea what part feels more natural to you? Are you more about listening, observing the situation, sensing what is going on? Or do you feel at ease while expressing yourself, putting yourself out there? Of course, these are not gender specific, but some philosophies see these two different parts as feminine and masculine energies. Every human being embodies both qualities, although not in the same amount.

What part feels most courageous to you?

Connecting with Talent receivers

What kind of shadow do we enlighten?
Before getting deeper into what it takes to connect authentically during Talent moments, it's important to know our receivers. Our Talent is specifically meant for a certain kind of situation. Our antenna comes with a wavelength for a certain kind of audience. Like in Paul's case, his environment needed *Adventure*. He described his receivers as hamstrung people. Remember Kimberley, whose Talent she characterized as *Matriarch*? She is the solution for people who need attention and care to thrive in a corporate world.

No, we are not the cure to everything. Although you might know people who express their opinions and ideas to everyone who has ears, as if they are lighting their candles in sunlight, if there is no real need for it, the real effect is zero.

Now think about it while keeping your Talent in mind. Who is on your list to elevate to the next level? Who, in your eyes, is in distress? What makes your heart ache? To what situations are you the solution? My teachers always asked, *"Who is on your hit list?"*

The challenge is to connect and approach those people with an open mind. It might hurt us to see people in situations like this in such a way that they might even scare us away. Their internal hassles are frustrating to see, but that is exactly why we are drawn towards them. Can we really stay present and connected? If we can't yet, it could be our connections that aren't clear of barriers. Our connections might still be influenced by our own needs and/or our judgments.

How creating clear connections leads to expressing hidden potential

I am sure we all would be able to express our Talent easily behind closed doors with no one present to receive it. We wouldn't be so busy with self-preservation. To really connect with others, courage is required. Lots of relationships are bothered by obstructions we placed ourselves during the course of our lives to make things easier or to avoid difficult emotions.

"Your task is not to seek for love, but merely to seek and find all the barriers within yourself that you have built against it." We can use Rumi's quote about Love to explain what it takes to establish high-quality connections for Talent interventions. Expressing our Talent without holding back entails mostly seeking and finding all the barriers within ourselves—barriers to avoid genuine connections. To connect on a deep level can feel intimate. It can also feel intimidating to show up with our realness uncovered, certainly when the other person(s) are still hiding theirs.

There is a lot to learn, and it'll improve all our connections immensely if we take the time to zoom in. The fact that the quality of our connections has a significant effect on workplace success is an interesting bonus. Jane Dutton, an organizational psychologist at University of Michigan, researches the effects of high-quality connections within organizations. They appear to be critical building blocks for revitalizing and engaging employees. High-quality connections make people feel more resilient when they encounter setbacks or frustrations, and teams work more cohesively.[65]

---

[65] Dutton, J. *Energize your Workplace: How to Create and Sustain High-Quality Connections at Work*. Jossey-Bass July 2003

To express our natural response without holding back, we can learn what our conditioned responses in relating with others look like. When the going gets tough, how does that affect your relationship with others? We constantly project our own emotions on people who aren't always real or realistic. These projections can make the relationship unequal and out of balance. I remember quite vividly how I couldn't make a genuine connection with one of my training participants.

One year later, I suddenly realized how this woman triggered an unresolved issue within me. Subconsciously, her powerful attitude made me place myself in the position of a child again. Her power made me remember my mother's dominance. My Talent had no chance of showing itself because this woman triggered my feelings of helplessness during my childhood of not knowing how to deal with my mother's dominant force. If you have difficulty connecting with people in your surroundings, you might want to ask yourself what this person triggers within you. Only when you recognize and acknowledge these triggers, are you able to let them go and create clear connections.

A lot of organizational and personal theories about relation dynamics teach us how our relationships tend to be unequal and obstructed. Most of the times, we tend to place ourselves either "above" others or "beneath" others.

"Above" behaviors: We place ourselves above others because we need the status to feel worthy. Our connections might be blurred by our competitive drives and our need to feel better than them.

Think of someone like Daniel, who had the tendency of criticizing or even ignoring people who couldn't keep the pace he was initiating. His patronizing cues were scaring off the people who had reasons to go slow. They couldn't keep up with Daniel's high pace. Daniel wasn't able to show any compassion because his judgments were covering everything and standing in the way of his natural response to create movement. In a training program, he learned about how the relationship dynamics were influencing his connections, and acknowledged his patronal tendencies. He realized how he usually placed himself above another. He noticed how this bottlenecked many of his relationships, not only at work. He created a dis-balance. People would either rebel in dealing with his strict manners or would obey out of fear, but that's not what he was after. He was after real and honest connections.

He also learned how his rules about how everyone should behave provided him with a sense of safety. Acknowledging that he had been in need of this safety as a child, he learned to understand that he could now make an adult choice. His eyes opened for the people who benefited from his Talent, the people who were stuck. And when he started to really connect with them, his eyes opened to their real struggles. As soon as his judgments faded, he was able to reach out and put them in motion naturally. His Talent, *Creating Pace*, was inspiring to his team and created the energy that was needed.

"Beneath" behaviors: We place ourselves beneath others because we long for recognition and reassurance. To receive compliments, we might act more insecure than we are. We withdraw ourselves from the stage because of our need to feel safe.

Think of someone like Stacey, who had the tendency to feel overemotional in case people were showing passive-aggressive signs. She took these signs very personally up to a point she often couldn't hold her tears. She couldn't look at these situations with a clear mind, and often felt victimized. Her victim-behavior either placed others in rescue mode or ignited their aggressiveness even more.

Then Stacey discovered her Talent: *Bringing what's underneath to the surface*. People on her hit list were acting passive aggressively because there was something going on underneath the surface that ignited their fears and anger. She learned to observe them with fresh and calm eyes. Stacey was surprised how her own tendency to change her position from an equal human being to a victimized one blurred her relationships. Without having to deal with her own emotions, she could finally add her value.

Both Daniel and Stacey's internal hassles stood in the way of expressing their hidden potential. The picture shows a brief overview of three different relation dynamics theories that describe the above and beneath behaviors: the Drama Triangle, Transactional Analysis, and Leary's Rose.

	DRAMA TRIANGLE	TRANSACTIONAL ANALYSIS	LEARY'S ROSE
ABOVE	Do you have the tendency to rescue?	Do you notice "parent-like"-tendencies such as being normative or authorative?	Are you highly competetive within relationships?
	CONNECTING AT EYE LEVEL - EQUAL RELATIONSHIP		
BENEATH	Do you often feel a victim of situations?	Do you notice "child-like" tendencies such as being unconfident more than average, passive? Or in contrast, being a rebel?	Are you highly dependent or withdrawn within relationships?

I am not providing these theories with the honor they deserve by not addressing them more deeply, but please look at the overview and take a constrained relationship in mind.

Then ask yourself, what might be your tendency in relating with the other person? Do you associate yourself more with the above tendencies in the overview or more with the beneath tendencies? Now, take your ultimate receiver in mind. What happens in relating with this person? Do you tend to place yourself above or beneath this person?

What both Daniel and Stacey eventually learned is to connect on an equal level with the people that receive their Talents, and that leads us to the next technique we can practice to make way for our Talents in challenging environments:

AUTHENTICITY ENABLER #5: CONNECTING AT EYE LEVEL

Connecting at eye level is important because it enables us to see with clear eyes. It enables us to not be disturbed by our own emotional hassles. Besides this, if we connect at eye level, we allow the other person to connect at the same level. We are not triggering any extra unequal behaviors, because when we place ourselves above someone else, we invite others to either compete and show above behaviors or to withdraw and automatically place themselves beneath. And vice versa.

In other words, by clearing ourselves of our unresolved needs, we clear the connection. By placing ourselves at eye level with our receivers, they no longer exist in order to provide us with status, recognition, or false love. We are ready to give our Talent.

Connecting on this level continues to be a life-long practice, I'm afraid. I still have to remind myself, when entering meeting rooms full of people wearing tough masks. I know they are wearing their masks for a reason, but I still am aware of my fear. I still am aware of my tendency to shrink and my desire to disappear from the stage. When I fail to make a good impression, I immediately know the reason. I didn't connect at eye level. I placed myself underneath, and *the real me* escaped the room before the meeting was done. My illusionary need to stay safe prevailed. Sure, I did what was expected, but I failed to make a real impact. When I make a good impression, I surely connected with myself first, felt compassion for their need to stay tough, felt ease with my own uneasiness, and connected with them at eye level. Establishing that equal connection allowed me to share my Talent and allowed them to recognize my added value.

The most essential roadblocks standing in the way of creating these connections are *our judgments*. They prohibit us from seeing what is really going on. Judgments stand in the way of our care and our empathy. They close us up and blur our connections. You might have heard lots of experts speaking about compassion, but have you ever felt the value of compassion in work situations?

Wouldn't it be wonderful if when someone approached you in a manipulating manner, you were instantly able to see the inability of that person? Instead of being blurred by your judgment about that person or a judgment about yourself lacking the ability to deal with it, what if your Talent could be switched on to answer this attack with nothing other than a caring gesture? Compassion is all about allowing our hearts to join what we are doing. When we start seeing with our hearts, our judgments start to fade. Our harsh opinions start to melt and we begin sensing the underlying reasons for ineffectiveness and inefficiencies. When our judgments are transformed into compassion, we can join the connection as *ourselves* and start seeing the other person(s) at eye level. Suddenly, all of the underlying reasons turn into information for our Talent to care for.

You might want to join *the one-day compassion experiment*. I challenge you to become aware of all the judgments you have, just for one day. You'll be amazed by the enormous amount of judgments that arise. Each time you catch a judgment, try to transform this roadblock into a compassionate thought. For example:
- *About others:* "That woman is so slow in responding to my team" into "I see that she responds slower than the others. I wonder what the reason is for her delay?"
- *About yourself:* "Oh, why did I miss that opportunity to make my statement?" into "Good thing I saw that opportunity. This time I didn't feel safe enough to jump in to share my opinion. Maybe next time?"

You'll start seeing our judgments are nothing more than ways to protect ourselves from connecting with others at eye level. Judgments disconnect us from the outside world. *You might be ready to establish genuine connections, aren't you?*

Expressing Talent without holding back

Reclaiming our space
"Failure isn't fatal, hesitation can be," Nurse Crane said at the end of an episode of the Netflix series *Call the Midwife*[66]. Her remark res-

---

[66] Netflix series, *Call the Midwife*, originally a BBC period drama based on a memoir by Jennifer Worth, July 2002

onated with me because I realize we are conditioned to think failure is fatal, so we don't try at all or hesitate to act. *"Should I or shouldn't I?"* Regrets are all we are left with, and regrets are fatal.

Take writing this book. It feels vulnerable to write a book and to tell friends about it because I'm not sure how it will all turn out. But I am enjoying the writing process. I enjoy sharing my knowledge and finding the right form for you to absorb it. I am fascinated by the research and creation part of it. What if I had still hesitated and kept hesitating for years? I would have encountered so many cues not to write a book. The idea would have been stuck in my head forever, paralyzing every move. Sure, I feel paralyzed sometimes in this process, but I am happy my will to write is larger than my fear and hesitation.

The last part of this book is all about putting our Talent into action and allowing yourself to take up space. *To just do it!* This is the moment to dig for the treasure and share the gold. After sensing our receivers, after we've shifted within and connected with ourselves, after we've waited for our creative hunches, it is time to act on those, whether they involves a three-second Talent intervention or a year-round Talent project. Because merely thinking about what a difference we could make is a waste of your value to make a real difference. Nelson Mandela said, "Vision without action is only dreaming" and "action without vision is wasting time," but "vision with action can change the world."

In doing so, we connect a very precious and original part of ourselves with the outside world. That's the exciting part—it's where we get to add our value. Where we get to share our natural response in what we are amazingly good at. Where we will find real connection, because *we* are in that magic moment without wearing our mask. It's where we get to make an impact with what really matters to us.

Sometimes, we let our unique value get smothered by others, and it's our task to regain our space. Sometimes, life lessons arrive in the form of people. My biggest "teacher" in taking full ownership of my own value was my former business partner, Guy. When he was in the room, you immediately knew. He was present and he "owned" the place. His presence left me fighting for my position.

As I was so used to fitting in, almost disappearing at times, I had to learn that I had the right to be present as well. He had the tendency to come really close, too close, at times. The frustration I built up during those times urged me to show up and regain my space. It's incredible how frustration can be fuel for change. When I became clear and figured out my own presence, he was more than willing to step back. He wasn't making sure I couldn't stand out, instead, I, myself, was preventing myself from standing out. I was hesitant and unclear.

Reclaiming my space was, and remains, a scary part. For such a long time, my Talent was safely hidden to the outside world and myself. But as I am driven to revitalize and to make a difference, I now know that the uneasiness of reclaiming my space often comes with expressing my Talent.

Debby followed a Talent Development program at my friend's organization, an amazing place where they create all the circumstances necessary to help each person's Talent blossom. Something shifted as Debby acknowledged she was an expert in something special. She was a born *Celebrator*. She worked at a governmental institute, and she could use her Talent in her current job. She transformed her team from unengaged to happy, productive workers because Debby knew how to celebrate successes and milestones. However, she had a secret dream to be a singer-songwriter.

In the Talent Development program, she openly admitted her dream for the first time and started to experiment with it. My friend immediately recognized her Talent and her singing and songwriting skills. She was touched by her Talent in such a way that when the fifth-year anniversary of her organization approached, she asked Debby to create a song to celebrate this anniversary with a bang. My friend had high expectations—this song should have the potential to reach the Top 40. Debby was excited and immediately said yes. A process of highs and lows kicked off.

She had three things in place: her Talent as a driving force, a specific time frame, and a team to help her. She started full of confidence and excitement, but as the time passed, she became more insecure. She created the first part of the song but questioned whether it was good enough. She decided to involve one of her friends, a music producer, because she figured he would know what to do. They started working together intensively. After a few weeks, my friend asked for an update. Debby burst into tears. The song wasn't there yet. It was a mess. She lost herself.

So, what happened? By asking her producer friend, she released all her ownership and handed it over to him. She trusted *his* experience over *her* Talent. She let her whole Talent disappear from the stage while trying to keep up with his cues. She lost her way; she lost her own track.

In this last part, we will zoom into aspects what it takes to "just do it" without losing track. What does it take to not be paralyzed by hesitation and have the courage to openly connect with the people that need our Talent? Taking full ownership of our Talent is important for enabling the effect it deserves. A hunch deserves to be followed through until crossing the finish line. We don't want to lose sight of it along the way and let it fade away. Therefore, the last technique to ease our uneasiness while standing out:

AUTHENTICITY ENABLER #6: TAKING FULL OWNERSHIP

Debby handed over all the ownership to her friend, the "expert." She gave all of her authority to his expertise along the way. Along that way, she lost her unique value and with that, the song she was asked to create lost its unique value. Debby almost ended up with a song with nearly nothing of herself in it. It might have been a professional song, but it wasn't infused with her Talent. Luckily, she regained her ownership in time. She explained to her producer friend what she expected from him. He admired her clarity and was happy to follow her leadership.

Owning your Talent interventions for the full 100 percent doesn't mean you can't include others to help you. It just means you have the lead and you keep the lead. If not, *your* value is not clear, and *your* vagueness blocks the people who wait to receive your Talent's value.

Turning the V from vague into the C from clear

Violist Rosanne Philippens started playing the violin at the age of three. Nowadays, she is an award-winning artist. When an interviewer asked her about people that made a difference in her career, she mentioned her teacher. When she was a child, she was playing pretty well but not brilliantly. Her teacher knew she was withholding herself. Her playing was vague, as in not clear. She was hesitant. As if she didn't take a stand, as if she didn't fully own her playing. After a lesson, the only thing her teacher had to say was, "It starts with a V," and Rosanne would know her teacher was referring to her vagueness. She knew that she had to give it all instead of only half.

The same applies for your Talent. If you have a hunch, you have to go for it for the full 100 percent. When you fully express your Talent without holding back, your Talent is extremely inspiring, motivational, and vital to your surroundings.

I remember one of the training programs that I facilitated. At some point, I found myself sitting all curled up, hands under my legs, head bowed, as if I wanted to disappear. I saw everything that was happening in the room and got hunches, but I didn't have the courage to act on them, so I was running a standard training program. As I sat on my chair, on my hands, I realized I was literally sitting on my Talent. I didn't own my space as a facilitator of the training.

That moment, where I saw myself sitting and sending "vague" vibes, I changed my bodily position. I sat up straight, took a fresh inhale, put my hands on my lap, and looked into the room with a fresh pair of eyes. I regained my responsibility and owned my responsibility. The difference was like night and day.

What about you? Do people ever have to remind you by saying, "it starts with a V"?

Being ourselves in a genuine connection

"Creativity is the encounter of the intensively conscious human being with his or her world," Rollo May wrote in his book *The Courage to Create*[1]. While acting on a Talent hunch, we create an intense connection with others, either brief or long. This intensity can scare us. Somehow, we lost the ability to really connect as ourselves with the rest of our world. A true connection is when two souls meet and experience a moment between two separate human beings. Two different human beings, but how often do we end up copying the other person in order to stay on the same track? We think alike, so we are connecting, right? But are we really? And if we don't agree with the other person, we tend to shield our authenticity out of fear and we close ourselves off. We are still debating, but a real connection is lost. The intensity of a genuine connection makes us want to flee.

A well-known training exercise is to look in each other's eyes and be silent for five to ten minutes. Immediately, this creates an awkward feeling. You know why? Because we normally instantly cover these intense feelings with smiles, random words, and gestures. Our authentic selves instantly want to escape from real connections. You might have endured the awkwardness and looked into each other's eyes without interference. You probably saw each other and you genuinely connected despite feeling too vulnerable.

Artist Marina Abramovic took this to the next level. She sat in the New York Museum for Modern Art for three months, inviting audience members to sit across from her and exchange gazes without any interruptions. People started to cry and felt immensely connected because of the focused attention and immense presence, which is rare in our scattered society. Lots of the visitors didn't dare to join this experiment of intense connection because it was too straightforward, too vulnerable, or too shocking.

What does it mean to connect as *yourself*? I remember a singing workshop where the value of "staying yourself within a connection" struck me for the first time. The trainer, Jan Kortie, invited two people to sing on stage. Of course, singing is something lots of people are embarrassed about, so the invitation to sing on stage resembled a way to perfectly get out of your comfort zone. At first, the two volunteers sang but their attempts to sing together and to follow each other's rhythm didn't lead to anything worthwhile.

It wasn't until Jan invited them to each sing with their own voice and asked them not to be seduced to follow the other person's voice. In other words, he invited them to sing and create from within instead of reacting to what the other person was singing. The moment they each sang with their own authentic voice was like time stood still. Their sounds were beautiful together. Their vulnerability created a transparency and honesty and, therefore, trust.

That's when it struck me—it really is more valuable if we stick to what we've got. Real connections are only possible when we show up as ourselves. Otherwise, you'll connect with my mask, which isn't me. Or you connect with your own mirror image, which might be nice, but you're really only connecting with a fake copy of yourself. The real value of the connection with another person lies in the fact that the other person is different. I would soon feel bored if there were only *Ankes* in this world, right?

In expressing our Talent, we express our *different* value to the other. Each Talent has its own challenge to stay different within that connection. Consider these two:

- *Just be and do nothing*: This book shares a lot of examples where a Talent enables a person to do something for someone else. But sometimes, for some people and their Talents, just being there and refraining from doing anything brings the most significance. Diana's Talent is a *Safe Haven*. Just by being herself, she is a *Safe Haven*. But Diana was programmed that "just being there" wasn't enough. She didn't do anything, so she didn't mean anything. "Doing nothing" made her connections with others feel incredibly uncomfortable. The silence and the absence of disturbance almost made the connection feel too intimate. Now, she understands that, in some cases, talking and doing things distract from her Talent's value. Even things she normally does when she comforts someone, distract. Luckily, she learned that overdoing can ruin the moment. Just being present and awake can be incredibly soothing and healing for people who benefit from her Talent.

- *Being honest*: Although all our Talents are actually little packages of Love, it doesn't always mean our Talent is being perceived as love right away. Emma's Talent is to *Observe*. Her observations are incredibly sharp and people aren't always ready to receive the harsh light of truth. The truth is not always convenient and since convenience is rooted in our Western society, we tend to look away from the underlying reality. Despite the fact that she learned to wrap her message in a way people were able to receive her Talent, the challenge to share her honest observations is still there. *Does your Talent challenge you in a specific way as well? And do you realize the true value of being this different to someone else?*

Rumi has a wonderful take on this:

Love comes with a knife, not with some shy question and not with fears for its reputation.

Owning our Power

Besides hiding ourselves because we think we are not good enough, we might be afraid of showing our immense strength. I remember my mother showing me Marianne Williamson's[67] poem. At that time, it didn't really resonate the same way that the poem resonated for her. Later in life, I realized that there is so much wisdom in this piece. Maybe I was afraid of being powerful and grand, instead of being afraid that I wasn't adequate?

> *...Our deepest fear is not that we are inadequate.*
> *Our deepest fear is that we are powerful beyond measure.*
> *It is our light, not our darkness that most frightens us.*
> *We ask ourselves, who am I to be brilliant, gorgeous, Talented, fabulous?*

Maybe I refrained my strength because I was afraid that it would crush others? Maybe I was so oversensitive of hurting other people's feelings that I gave other people more space instead of taking up my own?

> *Your playing small does not serve the world.*
> *There is nothing enlightened about shrinking so that other people won't feel insecure around you.*

---

[67] Marianne Williamson, *A Return to Love* (Harper Collins, 1992)

Among other things, the Dutch culture has taught me that keeping small is better than excelling—the tall puppy syndrome. To be honest, I always had a slight aversion to people who shine in the spotlight. I labeled this as egocentric. When someone is winning, there is always someone losing. And I didn't like to win if that meant someone was losing because of me. But does that really make sense?

> *And as we let our own light shine, we unconsciously give other people permission to do the same.*
> *As we are liberated from our own fear, our presence automatically liberates others.*

Standing out by expressing our Talent is the opposite of being egocentric; it's all about serving others, about having a positive impact—so everyone wins. A sentence that continues to be of value is: *I don't use my Talent to score; I use my Talent to touch.* The world is not improved by keeping ourselves small and staying aloof. We all are incredibly indispensable for the world around us, and we all are needed for something else.

Surfing on the waves of our Will

"Don't should yourself." This line on my spinning instructor's T-shirt is an incredibly wise statement, also in our case. Ask yourself: *Do I really want to stand out in significance? Is it a genuine desire or an extra demand I add to my list? Do I want to show up authentic despite my fears?*

I hope you have developed a deeper sense of wanting this, because our deeper will is the fuel for this kind of profound, although not always comfortable, change. It enables us to just do it, despite our fear, to have just the right amount of courage to jump in the pool backwards.

I realized my will can be larger than my fear during an exercise several years ago. We, the participants, entered our training room and the setup was different. The room was transformed in one huge arena marked off with tape, surrounded by chairs at each side. After our teacher explained the exercise, everyone became silent. There would be two people meeting each other in the arena while being watched by us, the audience. Not meeting in the sense of "Hi, how are you doing?" No, this was a whole different ballgame. She asked us to really meet each other—to make genuine contact. No masks allowed, no conditioned greetings, solely pure and authentic contact. Our only resources would be our creativity and our authenticity.

The first couple was invited into the arena. They took place opposite each other. One person slowly walked to one corner of the arena and turned her back to the other person. The other person took a few slow steps as if she was consciously trying to sense the other person's vibes. She decided to sit on the floor a few steps behind her, keeping her eyes closed. The person in the corner took this as an invitation to turn herself, and she also took a seat on the floor, with her eyes still closed. As soon as they both opened their eyes, everyone in the room felt it. This was real genuine contact between two authentic souls. It was incredibly beautiful to watch. Goosebumps.

Another couple was invited to the arena, and another couple, and so forth. Some couples took 10 minutes, others only a few seconds. I was in the audience waiting to be chosen as part of the next couple and felt my heart beating loud and fast. I was deadly scared by this exercise. The idea of being in that arena where I was supposed to strip my mask off felt naked. Then, suddenly, one of the participants asked if she could use the restroom and that was our teacher's cue to end this exercise. What?! According to her, it had been so intense that there was no energy left to finish this activity. I was astonished and frustrated.

After everyone took a short break, she asked what each one of us had learned, even if we didn't take part of the actual exercise. Luckily, this question transformed my frustration into an insight because after I put my astonishment aside, I realized something huge. I desperately wanted to do this exercise despite my trembles and fears. I realized and felt in my bones "that my will is larger than my fear." This insight never left my mind. It might have been more powerful than doing the actual exercise.

When you find yourself in an environment that doesn't naturally invite you to show your authentic self, inspire yourself by asking, "Is my will larger than my fear?" At times when you feel that inner drive to make a difference, let yourself be carried by the waves of your will. In a sense, the expression of our Talent is comparable with surfing. When you find yourself in a situation where you can make a difference, wait for the right wave to arrive and jump on your board with determination despite any cutbacks in control. Stand up with your eyes focused straight ahead to hold your balance, in other words— own this Talent intervention—and enjoy the freedom that comes with expressing your authenticity.

To carry on with the surfing analogy, riding the waves feeling free requires practice. For such a long time, we used to do everything by the book, so it feels uncomfortable to stand out and do things differently. Reaching the last pages of this book, I hope you have worked your way through each of the Authenticity Enablers. Each in their own way, these enablers provide you with a sense of ease with the uneasiness of expressing yourself. Especially in moments when it matters.

If we want to keep catching the right waves and expressing our Talent to the fullest, we will have to practice:

- To disconnect from the outside world to connect with ourselves using meditation (*#1: Disconnecting to connect*).
- To turn the tide and become masters of our own time instead of feeling slaves of our calendar. Owning our own time allows us to experience flow and feel inspired to make a difference (*#2: Owning our time, otherwise it'll own us*).
- To tread new ground using our curiosity as a compass (*#3: Escaping our fixed reality boxes by unleashing our curiosity*).
- To value our vulnerabilities and experience the freedom of choosing something different in order to make a difference (*#4: Daring to fall in order to fly*).
- To connect at an equal level to establish genuine contact instead of letting our emotional hassles disturb our authentic Talent interventions (*#5: Connecting at eye level*).
- To see an opportunity to express our Talent in a challenging situation, we can practice taking full ownership and not letting our doubts or other people take over (*#6: Taking full ownership*).

Authenticity Enablers:

#1: Disconnecting to connect

#2: Owning our time, otherwise it'll own us

#3: Escaping our fixed reality boxes by unleashing our curiosity

#4: Daring to fall in order to fly

#5: Connecting at eye level

#6: Taking full ownership

To put this book into practice, I suggest the following:

1. Ask yourself this question: *what Authenticity Enabler is most challenging for me at this moment?*

2. Focus on this enabler for the coming month:
    - Add this enabler to your calendar to remind yourself each day, and gather all insights you'll receive on the way.
    - Read the chapter about this Authenticity Enabler again, reflect, do the exercises, and make notes.
    - The last day of the month, take 10 minutes to reflect: *what is the most important insight I learned while focusing on this Authenticity Enabler?* This way, you will subtract the most important knowledge to integrate this into daily life.
    - Write your most important insight on a card and place it where you can see it daily.

3. The first day of the next month, pick another Authenticity Enabler and repeat all the steps.

Just remember to surf on the waves of your Will. Your desire to express yourself and to make a difference will guide you to enter "the Arena despite your doubts." Please remember that not one person gets to enable themselves over night. So I hope you keep practicing these enablers to create the courage to be authentic at work.

You might have heard Theodore Roosevelt's speech, *A Man in the Arena*. I am happy to share this here with you in the hope it encourages you even more to enter your Arena.

A Man in the Arena

It is not the critic who counts; not the man who points out how the strong man stumbles, or where the doer of deeds could have done them better.
The credit belongs to the man who is actually in the arena, whose face is marred by dust and sweat and blood; who strives valiantly; who errs, who comes short again and again, because there is no effort without error and shortcoming; but who does actually strive to do the deeds; who knows great enthusiasms, the great devotions; who spends himself in a worthy cause; who at the best knows in the end the triumph of high achievement, and who at the worst, if he fails, at least fails while daring greatly, so that his place shall never be with those cold and timid souls who neither know victory nor defeat.

All the luck with standing out in significance. Your face might be "marred by dust and sweat and blood." You might stumble, but at least you won't have regrets. At least you will have stories of fulfillment to tell in your retirement home. At least you will get to share your Talent in abundance.

Thank you for turning your world into a better place. Thank you for your Talent!

Acknowledgements

Sure, I am proud my name is on this book's cover. How cool is that? I recognize the mix of happiness and relief I felt after graduating and seeing my name on the cover of my thesis. But, to be honest, the cover should be 10 sizes bigger to fit all the names that contributed to the origination and conclusion of this creative act. I am truly grateful for all the Talents that affected me, each in their own specific way.

First of all, ballet dancer Michael Linsmeier, your Talent was the first spark to light the fire to write this book. Your way of dancing expressed "Give it all you got!" and so I did. Thank you!

What would I have done without the teachers I've met along my own, still-continuing journey to expressing my Talent without holding back? Thank you, Ad Maas, Britt B Steele, Charlotte Oosterhoff, Desiree Wennekes, Erica de Dreu, Jan de Dreu, Jouke Post, Marianne Broos. And Jalaluddin Mevlana Rumi also has a place as one of my teachers, as I find continuous inspiration in his poems. To you all: I bow to you and thank you for dedicating your life to my and many others' journeys towards freedom.

I would like to thank all the people I met in training programs and coaching sessions. Your struggles and epiphanies provided me with this book's theme and taught me that the delicate balance between fitting in and standing out is of great importance. Thank you for confiding in me and absorbing my Talent the way that you do.

Although I tend to appreciate long periods of deep concentration and flow, writing can be a lonely act. But I didn't feel alone in this project at all. The pre-readers of this book plowed through the first concepts. An Claes, Bastiaan Sommeling, Bernadet Bos, Bernadet Haveman, Holly Amaoko, Jeanet Schouten, Karlijn De Broeck, Kristin Hibler, Mary Sommerset, Miranda Huiden, Ramya Rajagopal, and Tamara Hofman, thank you so much for your time, commitment and honest feedback, each in your own wonderful way. Then my editors, Kelly Lamb and Margarita Martinez: it's amazing how you are able to improve my sentences and still make me think I wrote it. Holly Amaoko (book cover and illustrations) and Chelsea Perri (pictures, in this book and my blog), thank you for being my besties here in the US. Your creativity and willingness to help out make my day. My mentors, Ellen Weustink and Godelieve Meeuwissen: You walked by my side during this process so that I could lean on you when needed. You are the living proof that everyone who starts and wants to finish a creative project should benefit from having true companions like you.

Lieve Pappa and Mamma, I truly appreciate the foundation your upbringing provided me with, as well as the continuous enthusiasm you both display when I tell you about what's on my mind.

Lieve Yannick and Raphael, your endless wisdom is a source of inspiration. I truly hope you both stay as true to yourselves as you can. Lieverds, this world deserves your value!

Lieve Mark, without you, this book would have been nothing more than an idea. Traveling the world together with you means the world to me.

This book really is an accomplishment for us all. Thank you for your Talent,

Anke

Beyond the Book

Staying in tune with your Talent needs practice, certainly in the beginning. Expressing your authenticity and wholeheartedness is courageous and we, life-long learners, can benefit from going on this journey together.

It's my mission to facilitate people in making a real difference in their world. Therefore, I offer four ways[68] to enable clients to stay engaged, inspired, and motivated to express their authenticity.

Talent in 1 Word (7 days)

Join the online program *Your Talent in 1 word* if you want to deepen your understanding of your Talent. Each day during one week, you will receive a simple exercise to clarify your understanding of your Talent. You will gain confidence and learn to own your newly identified Talent. As a reader of this book, you are entitled to join this program for free. More information on: www.anketusveld.com/mytalent

Talent Intensive (7 weeks)

If you want to work closely with me, or another certified Talent expert, and want to deepen your understanding of your Talent, subscribe to the *Talent Intensive*. During these seven weeks, you zoom in on both sides: your tendencies that prohibit you from being who you are, as well as your Talent. Step by step, the Talent expert will encourage you to take leaps and experiment with your Talent. At the end, you'll understand the value and effect of your Talent and what you personally need in order to use it without holding back. You can find more information at: www.anketusveld.com/talentintensive

---

[68] These offers are subject to change. Find more information: www.anketusveld.com

Program *Authentic Leadership Enabled* (7 months)

Apply for this intensive seven-month program if you want to integrate the learning of this book, if you want to abundantly express your Talent in challenging situations, and increase your leadership presence. If you have a preference for working 1-on-1, I offer an individual program in which we alternate online coaching and reflective exercises.

Also, I facilitate small groups to learn and experiment together using real and specific work- and life-related challenges. Kindred spirits who want to share, learn, and create insights in an encouraging learning setting. You can find more information at: www.anketusveld.com/authenticleadershipenabled

Talent Inspiration (Year-round)

Subscribe to my *Talent Inspiration* emails if you are looking for inspiration, reminders, and encouragement each week for one year. Go to: www.anketusveld.com/talentinspiration

ABOUT THE AUTHOR

An expert on Talent and Authentic Leadership, Anke Tusveld has facilitated hundreds of people towards becoming authentic, innovative, and confident leaders. People who make a difference and who are able to connect on a deeper level in a fast-paced, demanding corporate culture.

The founder of an Innovation Agency and an executive trainer and coach at *de Baak*, one of the most renowned leadership institutes in Europe, Anke has worked for Global Fortune 500 companies, as well as with entrepreneurs and nonprofits to rediscover and maximize the Talents of leaders and their teams.

Anke holds a Master's of Science in Innovation Management and is a Certified Talent Coach. With her husband and two sons, she has lived on three continents for the past five years and is immensely enjoying the differences and similarities between the different cultures.